# ALL ROADS LEAD INWARD

*My Spiritual Journey of Healing, Self-Empowerment, and Surrendering to My Soul's Purpose*

JENNIFER VROOM

ALL ROADS LEAD INWARD



ISBN: 979-8-9922207-6-6

Book Design by Transcendent Publishing
Editing by Dana Micheli
Photography by Jennifer Vroom
Photo Credit: Anthony James Higginbottom

The author has made every effort to faithfully recreate events, locations, and conversations from her memories. To protect the privacy of individuals, she may have changed names, locations, and, in some cases, altered certain identifying details and characteristics.

Printed in the United States of America.

*"If light is in your heart, you will find your way home"*

**~Rumi**

# DEDICATION

This book is intended to offer inspiration to anyone who feels afraid or stuck in their lives…

Anyone whose SOUL CRAVES FREEDOM from the confines of their current situation, from the programming of society, and from the expectations or judgments of others…

Those who have bypassed the logical route for the one that is guided by their heart…

Those gypsy spirits and nomads like me, who will take the leap of faith and will always take the road less traveled, even when the road is foggy and you can't see what's ahead of you…

Those who will muster the courage within to take that first step, be brave enough to move past the fear every time it creeps up, and then be patient enough to allow each small step to be revealed one at a time trusting that the next one will appear just when you need it.

This is the road that will lead you back home… to your TRUE SELF.

When it seems like you're lost or alone, you need only to pause and tune into your own inner compass, your internal GPS, and it will guide you home every single time…

To reconnect with and embody your soul's true purpose.

# PROLOGUE

Most of us, at some point, are faced with a crossroads and must make a choice that's scary and difficult. The truth is that we don't have a choice at all. The crossroads is the moment you realize you can no longer deny that something is missing from your life – something you cannot live without because it is the whole reason you are here. You may not be able to put a name to it, yet you've felt it nagging at you for months, years, or even decades; now, you must leap into the unknown and follow your soul's calling. That is where I found myself when at age forty-six I made the heart-wrenching decision to end my twelve-year relationship, give away almost all my belongings, and venture out on a solo five-month road trip with my inner guidance as the only GPS.

That's what this story is about – stepping into the abyss and just trusting that all will work out. When I took this step, I had been a Speech-Language Pathologist for twenty-three years. Though it was rewarding in many ways, I always knew deep down it was not the work I was supposed to be doing. My excuse for remaining was the time I had already invested, including six years of higher education; plus, I had tried other things that didn't pan out. And yet, something else was definitely calling me. I didn't exactly know what that "something else" would look like, but I knew it would involve teaching and helping to empower people, because this was at the core of all my life's work, whether I was working with students with special needs or the adult in the skilled nursing facility who'd just had a stroke and wanted to get back some basic life skills we take for granted.

For several years I had also been teaching meditation and mindfulness. It had been my saving grace in my teen years, lifting me out of a deep depression, and continued to be helpful ever since. And yet, I still had so much more to learn. The year 2016 brought a huge wakeup call in the form of hospitalizations and surgeries, cause unknown. As the doctors had no solution, I was forced to go within and, with meditation and my intuition, find the answers to my healing. This experience inspired me to form my company, Evoke Meditation, so I could share my lifelong meditation practice with others. I also began to understand that what I always thought was just good common sense and strong emotional intelligence went beyond the typical sensitivity and intuition most people are able to tap into. What followed was an active exploration and opening up of my psychic and mediumistic skills, which I had always respected in others but never imagined I possessed.

The more I opened this new door, the clearer everything in my life became. When I looked at my career, my relationship, and my purpose from a broader perspective, I realized the degree to which I had been denying who I really was – and adhering to "normal" standards to avoid judgment. Despite my mom's best efforts to convince me I should be married with kids, living comfortably in a suburban home, I was always searching for another route. My family and friends always knew I was "different," but since I was independent and functioning in a way that made sense to them, all was kosher. Even my partner had flippantly commented that I "wasn't exactly the litmus test for normal." Such true words! Yet I didn't feel comfortable "coming out" to him or anyone else about my gifts and how my day-to-day experience with the world seemed very different from what I observed in others. When the realization hit, it hit hard and could not be ignored. The life I had created was not honoring my true self and was certainly not utilizing the gifts I'd come into the world with. It was time to take that other route I had been seeking. *If not now,* I asked myself, *when?*

The following weekend, I sat down with Jared, my partner of twelve years, and explained why I needed to leave him and our home. I was going to give my full attention and focus to my spiritual journey, including my psychic and mediumistic work. I wished I had been given the latitude and support to share this with him sooner; however, based on past conversations and things he had said, it was pretty clear that he didn't believe in any of this woo-woo stuff. Even in a standard yoga class, Jared would get annoyed if the instructor made any spiritual or esoteric references. If I tried to bring up some of my observations or experiences, they were dismissed. More importantly, throughout our relationship all my time and effort was spent nurturing and supporting him and his daughters, of whom he had shared custody since his divorce. My needs were always last on the list, though I take full credit for allowing that to be the case all those years. I knew that with all he had on his plate he just didn't have anything extra to give. I also knew, deep down, that if I asked more of our already fragile relationship, it would have crumbled a lot sooner.

Jared and I weren't married, but I had devoted myself to him as if we were. Leaving certainly felt like a divorce, though fortunately not nearly as messy. Most importantly, we didn't have the drama that often comes with a split because we were both able to see each other with love and appreciation for the time we shared.

There I was, at the young age of forty-six, venturing out on my own after more than a decade. I have never had any tie to material items, so I was okay walking away from the home we'd designed and built together with just the basic essentials and a few family heirlooms. I donated the rest of my belongings, then moved into my parents' guest room for a couple of weeks while I developed a plan on where to go and what to do.

In the end, my "plan" turned out to be not much of one at all. Since I knew I was ready to go all-in on the next phase of my spiritual journey but had little clarity on what that entailed, I decided to simply take my gypsy spirit on the road, stopping at one waystation at a time while trusting that my intuition would guide me along the way.

My first stop would be Asheville, North Carolina. Next stop ... who knows?

BEACH ACCESS
SILVER SANDS BEACH

## CHAPTER ONE

# SACRIFICE

***"Powerful achievements are usually born as a result of great sacrifice. By surrendering and letting go, there will be more room to receive."***

**~ by John Holland**
**The Psychic Tarot Oracle Deck**

# DAY ONE

## Asheville, NC

***"A thousand miles begins with a first step."***

**~ Lao Tsu**

After my Saturday mediumship group this morning, which offered me some perfectly timed and much-needed messaging and encouragement, I kissed my folks goodbye at their Fayetteville home and headed for the mountains.

I had an amazing playlist of songs, inspired by my friend, Michael, that I'd been listening to nonstop for the past few weeks. Michael Bodine is an extremely gifted Psychic, Ghostbuster, Author, and Speaker; in fact, we hit it off after I scheduled a reading with him. It was one of those readings that goes beyond mundane questions to become a catalyst for transformation. It woke me up from the slumber I'd allowed myself to fall into for so long; it made me see how I'd allowed my soul to take a back seat to everyone's needs.

Indeed, Michael's reading was different, and I would know, having been drawn to psychics, mediums, numerology, astrology, dream interpretation – anything metaphysical – since my teen years. I was looking for an alternative perspective to help make sense of this physical "reality"; I also got readings as a way to check in and get confirmation of my own intuition. Eventually, I started offering my own psychic and mediumship readings – a practice I had dived deeper into over the past couple of years. Therefore, I took messages from other readers with a grain of salt and always tapped in for myself to see what nuggets resonated with me and what I would leave behind.

One of these past readings stands out in stark relief. I was on the cusp of deciding whether to move in with my partner – something the intuitive advised me to reconsider. I was meant, they said, for a path toward "enlightenment" and more of a solitary soul journey. They also said this relationship was going to be a challenging one. Though I knew it was true, I also strongly felt it was worth the effort; I believed my partner and I still had more to learn from and give to one another.... .it didn't feel complete.

I wasn't sure if it was the timing, or if I was just more ready and willing to hear it, but Michael's message hit home. Everything he said rang so true, as if he could see right through any outer facade and straight into my soul.

"You're not normal, honey," he said, "and you're not gonna be normal. You and I are cut from the same cloth."

This wasn't new information; it was confirmation. Michael was speaking what I had been sensing for some time and my soul had been trying to get me to see for much longer than that. When someone sees you so clearly, they reflect it back to you like looking into a mirror. You truly see yourself, maybe for the first time ever, and you can no longer deny the truth of who you are.

Days after my reading, as much as I tried, I could not stop thinking about what was discussed. I couldn't shake the thought that I needed to make some major changes and movement in my life to allow my soul's purpose to unfold... to fulfill what I had always known deep down that I'd come here for in this incarnation.

Over the past week, I had been preparing for the launch of my road trip with excitement and anticipation, but this was sprinkled with moments of fear, uncertainty, and uneasiness. I felt unbalanced and even a bit numb at times. A daily run or hike helped, grounding me in the comforting arms of nature while inspiring music played through my earbuds. I also started listening to funny podcasts and watching uplifting movies, using laughter as medicine to help me find my balance through these uneasy feelings. I spent extra time attuning myself in meditation and connecting with my spirit guides to raise my vibration and surround me with healing and protective energies.

Now, as I drove toward Asheville, I thought about the message, received in that morning's mediumship group from my grandmother on the other side, that both validated my efforts and offered additional advice:

*"Sometimes precision is important, but other times you need more flexibility and to be more general.*

*Right now, just go with the flow.*

***Leave the faucet running.***

*Just let it be and allow yourself to get acclimated with things without needing a precise answer.*

*Let things move naturally without forcing it."*

Clearly I needed to continue focusing my energy on ME and getting myself back into alignment and balance. Be more flexible in how I perceived my life – and how I "needed" or wanted it to look like right now.

Shortly after this thought, I saw a sunflower on a passing car, which for me represents a sign from Spirit that they were with me and supporting me.

## (ANOTHER) DARK NIGHT OF THE SOUL

I had an easy, relaxing evening. After a nice warm shower, I meditated and connected with my spirit guides for a good hour. It felt wonderful. These sittings have become increasingly full of power, light, connection, support, and guidance; and, over the past week, I'd been sensing a new spirit guide. She was there almost as a psychic guide, but she also told me that we were family from previous lives. She usually appeared in front of or next to me with her hand on my arm, a comforting smile, and magical, lit-up eyes telling me it's okay...

After a simple dinner, I treated myself to doing nothing but watching a movie with popcorn and wine! The film I chose, *Breaking Dawn Part 2,* was not only a guilty pleasure but apropos considering Bella had just transitioned from her human life into a badass, supernatural version of herself. It reminded me of my meditations as of late, when while expanding my light and power I became as bright as a sun. Often, I transformed into a huge phoenix – reborn, more powerful and in tune with the Universe than ever.

While watching the movie, I began plotting a new course and looking at the map to determine where to go next. Just then, a thought popped into my head: I should see where and when Abraham-Hicks might be speaking. As soon as my eyes landed on an April 1 in-person event, the decision was made. I was headed for Phoenix!

After the movie, though, I felt a sudden, very unexpected wave of sadness come over me. I began to cry...then weep uncontrollably. The sadness was so deep and I had pushed it down over the last few weeks because I didn't really feel I had a safe space to deal with it. Now, as I sat alone in this Asheville Airbnb, it was forcing its way up and out.

I have always liked and needed some time to myself, but I didn't want to live a lonely life... again. I was sure I've lived past lives like this, when I felt different and isolated. Now, I cried for feeling frightened and alone. I cried for all the people who had hurt or disappointed me. I cried for the complete lack of control in my life and not knowing what the hell I was doing! I cried for always being denied a passionate, loving, nurturing relationship, which I needed now more than ever as I tried to navigate this new path.

Then, as I stood up and got ready to crawl into bed and cry myself to sleep, the sadness and grief for the loss of my old self, my relationship, and a safe, "normal" life turned quickly into anger … then rage. Moments from my past came bubbling up. I was so angry thinking of my childhood and how difficult it had been. Angry for being dropped into this crazy world and having to deal with stressful situations that pushed me to my limits from my earliest years and never seemed to stop. I was angry at Jared for never stepping up as the loving partner I wanted and needed, how he always put me last and never appreciated me until I finally told him after twelve years that I was leaving. I was angry at the college kid who raped me, stealing away my virginity, when I was eighteen. I was angry about feeling abandoned by my spirit team in my greatest times of need… Man, once the floodgates open, you see how much old stuff you've been still holding onto that you thought you were done with! It seems there's always another layer of the onion to peel back.

I began angrily whispering aloud, cognizant that I had to be quiet in this guest room (aka basement) so as not to awaken anyone in the house.

"I HATE YOU! I AM SO F*#!ING ANGRY AT YOU!!"

After half-crying, half-whisper-yelling at all those people from my past, I turned my attention and anger to my spirit guides and helpers and to God.

"I AM SO ANGRY AT YOU FOR ALL OF THIS!!! Why does it always have to be so hard?!"

This experience wasn't new to me. I've had many dark nights of the soul in my life, starting at a very young age. The stresses experienced by military families are different from others due to the constant possibility of any of the following: 1) being stationed somewhere new – and having to leave your home and friends behind, 2) deployment, when the soldier is sent on assignment without his/her family, and 3) TDY, ("temporary duty), which is basically the military version of a work assignment away from your current station, lasting up to one hundred eighty days. My dad once left us for a whole year on what is called a hardship deployment tour in Korea, and let's just say it ended up being much "harder" than we could have anticipated.

Also, many military parents have a different level of rules, expectations, and discipline than the average family. My older sister and I grew up in a very strict, demanding, and unforgiving household. What seemed like minor infractions to us were considered worthy of a potent trifecta of physical, mental, and emotional punishment. If we accidentally spilled a glass of milk, came home late, scraped our knee, or came home with anything but straight A's, we feared the consequences. Our mom, who was from Korea, didn't speak much English, lacked confidence, and felt alone, scared, and essentially trapped into parenthood. You can imagine what it was like to grow up in that kind of environment – let alone a child as sensitive and empathic as me.

There were times when Mom threatened to leave me and my sister. I recall as a young child feeling completely distraught as she phoned extended relatives about making arrangements to send us away for misbehaving. On another occasion, I hysterically begged her to stay as she marched out the door and headed down the street. She returned, but the message was clearly received. We were being reminded just how easy it would be for her to abandon us if we didn't stay in line. I remember feeling scared to be left alone and feeling horrible for never being worthy of love and acceptance from my parents.

Nighttime brought no respite, as I was plagued with nightmares and afraid of the dark and things that may be lurking there. Sometimes, I was so terrified I would ask to sleep in my parents' bed, even though I knew my mom would be pretty pissed off for being woken up. There were many accounts of my sleepwalking – no doubt my soul was taking a leave of absence to clear and replenish itself from all the stress and dense energy I endured during waking life. As early as I can remember, I never felt safe in any environment. I felt as though I always had to be on high alert and couldn't trust anyone around me.

By fifth grade I was so tired of the bullshit that I wanted to run away. We were stationed in Berlin, and though it was a vast improvement from our experience in Fayetteville, North Carolina, not everything had changed for the better. I felt disconnected from everything and everyone, including my family, classmates, and teachers. No matter how good my intentions were and how positive and loving I tried to be, people, and situations around me always felt unstable, unsupportive, imbalanced, and chaotic. I didn't understand how people could be so cold and unkind to one another. I always felt so vastly different, not just in my outer appearance, but in my way of thinking. And though my mixed race certainly had me stand out like a sore thumb, I knew it was much more than that since I felt like a stranger within my own family. I felt highly misunderstood and surrounded by a sea of negativity that I couldn't wrap my head around.

I never felt good in my body either. I remember sitting in front of a mirror in elementary school and clawing at my face, wanting to escape this physical vessel, and the world, I felt trapped in. I was exhausted from the weight of all the expectations I could never seem to live up to and from always having to live to a higher standard in order to feel any semblance of acceptance and love. I was sick and tired of having to always dance for my dinner, so to speak. Basically, it was a hard lesson in unconditional love from the perspective of not having it.

I remember being so angry at God-Source, and having the same kind of conversation I was having now, decades later. By age ten I had already experienced enough stress to ignite an overwhelming anger. I remember feeling as though someone had just dropped me off and left me here in this strange world to figure it all out on my own – a raw deal, for sure. I didn't think I was a bad person, so what had I done to deserve this?! As if my pain and isolation weren't enough, they were covered by a thick layer of guilt for feeling and talking that way to God. I remember for a long stretch after that first "break-up" with God, crying myself to sleep almost every night. This was how I spent much of my younger years, with fear, sadness, confusion, and anger my constant companions.

As a child, my sensitivities heightened as a way to protect myself; however, this also made me susceptible to dense or low-vibrational energies that would invade my space. I was incapable of setting boundaries, which led me to shut down emotionally to everyone around me. In my teen years, the dark energies, fear-based thoughts and feelings really pervaded my experience. That's when the panic attacks began, surrounding the true nature of reality versus the one the collective world had constructed and bought into hook, line, and sinker. I felt like Neo in *The Matrix* after he takes the red pill, but there wasn't a team to walk me through the awakening. I just freaked out quietly, on my own. My parents would have thought I was nuts and sent me to therapy, prescribed meds, had me committed, or all of the above! For me, the worst part was the thought that they, like everyone and everything around me, weren't real. It was ALL an illusion.

I guess you could say I came into this life a little different...

It's no wonder that as a teenager I was deeply depressed and suicidal, barely surviving junior high and high school. My higher self devised an ingenious strategy to trick my ego mind: each night I would bargain with myself, saying, *"If you just get through the next day, you can reward yourself by killing yourself the next night... just live one more day..."* I basically just put my head down and put one foot in front of the other, taking one little baby step at a time up that steep mountain until, finally, I found a place of relief.

Isn't it interesting how we always remember the bad stuff more than the good? It wasn't as if every moment of my childhood was bad. My parents were hardworking, honest people with high ethical standards and hearts of gold, doing the best they could and, like everyone else, figuring it out as they went. I also have many happy memories of our times together. But that's the way it works with healing and releasing patterns and memories that block or inhibit our fullest potential. If all the memories were joyful, you would want to hold onto them.

Now, for some reason I couldn't quite grasp, I was reliving all these raw feelings. I lay in bed and put my earbuds in, thinking I'd listen to something to help calm me. I didn't want the help of my spirit guides tonight, but I needed something – ANYTHING – to ease the pain. I listened to Tibetan bowls and just cried, releasing more sadness and anger that had been buried.

I knew that all of this pent-up pain and heart-wrenching emotion needed to be released, so I just let it all come up and out. ~Better out than in~

I now understood the recent advice to "leave the faucet running and let things flow naturally." It meant to allow the feelings to flow so I could cleanse and heal.

***This is the not-so-glamorous but crucial step in the awakening process: releasing what no longer serves you in order to open you up for everything to come. What so many don't realize is that when you numb yourself to the pain, you also numb yourself to true happiness.***

***Be brave enough to face the storm to get to the rainbow on the other side. The storms will pass; they are temporary, but necessary.***

## DAY TWO

Waking up, I recalled some weird, unsettling dreams that were obviously a product of the negative emotions that had emerged just before bed.

I could hear the rain on the red metal roof. According to the forecast it was supposed to continue all day, making it the perfect opportunity to take it easy, write, do art, plan, and maybe attend a yoga class or online spiritual service.

As usual, I didn't get out of bed until I did my morning meditation. I began by apologizing to my Spirit Team and God-Source for the angry words last night. I told them I understood that I'm on a more solitary path and reaffirmed my commitment to do the work I came here to do. This reminded me of when, as a teenager, I watched *Gorillas in the Mist* and felt so inspired by Dian Fossey. I could relate to her devotion to a greater purpose, even if it meant great sacrifice.

In my meditation, I felt a beautiful and powerful energy filling me up completely. I was empowered once again and expanded into a sun, a bright powerful light traveling out to the Multiverse.

## ASHEVILLE SALT CAVE

Needing some self-care and pampering, I made an appointment at the Asheville Salt Cave. Immediately, I was able to dive deep; in fact, at one point during the meditation I lost consciousness, surely out of my body. My hands began to heat up and I could feel energy moving inside me, starting in my head then moving to other areas. It was incredible, and the forty-five minutes flew by way too fast!

Afterward, I still felt airy and ungrounded as I stopped by Whole Foods to pick up dinner. I was in my own world and not really connecting with anyone (or wanting to). Once I realized this, I did make a better effort to look at people and reconnect to the physical world.

Once home, I extended my stay in Asheville by one day. I definitely wanted to return to the salt cave for more grounding to balance the spiritual work. I then did another meditation to connect with my spirit guides. I started to apologize again but they said there was no need. They love me unconditionally. There's nothing to forgive. I could see and feel several of my guides step forward to give me reassurance and words of wisdom. They told me I was on track and to just keep doing what I was doing, for now.

The words **Surrender, Trust, Let Go, Believe** were given to me. I was reminded to envision the outcome I want and to BELIEVE AND KNOW IT'S COMING and ON THE WAY.

**We are all so supported and it's so important to acknowledge and share our love and appreciation to our team of unseen helpers.**

I then pulled out The Psychic Tarot Oracle Deck by John Holland, shuffled, and got the "SACRIFICE" card:

> ***"Powerful achievements are usually born as a result of great sacrifice. This card represents... a time when you should look around your life to see what needs to be released. By surrendering and letting go, there will be more room to receive. The rewards for this are transformation, wisdom, gratitude, and enlightenment."***

## DAY THREE

It was hard to believe this was only the third day of my trip! It felt much longer.

During my morning meditation, I saw my psychic spirit guide holding my hands and linking fingers with me. She said I was family and I felt such love and support emanating from her. At the end of the meditation, I briefly fell into what felt like a deep, sleep-like state; likely, I was stepping out of my body for a well-needed break from the heaviness of the physical.

When I returned, I decided to listen to something fun that would ground me as I got ready. Lately, I'd been obsessed with the *SmartLess* podcast, and this morning the special guest was one of my favorites, Will Ferrell!

~Laughing is truly medicine for my soul~

After preparing for work, I came across an inspiring (and very timely) video about not forcing things and trying to make them happen the way you think they should, but rather preparing so you're in a place of readiness for what's to come. I was receiving the "Leave the faucet running" message again, just in a different way.

**Trust, believe, have faith that everything is being orchestrated on my behalf and to let it go for now.**

I thanked the Universe for always giving me the time and leverage to get my work tasks done easily, and for all their guidance. Boy, did I need it right now! I felt like I was in a trust fall. This wasn't an "I want or have to know what's going to happen next because I'm a control freak" scenario, but one a bit more extreme, considering:

- I didn't have a home.
- I didn't know where I'd be living by the end of the week.
- I'd just ended a significant relationship I had hoped would last a lifetime.
- I was in a job not really aligned with my purpose, but I wasn't sure exactly what I was supposed to be doing.

There was no going back to my old life and I didn't know what was waiting for me around the next corner. I just knew I felt a strong magnetic pull toward some new path and had to trust where it was going to take me.

**I'm just taking everything one step,**
**one intuitive whisper, at a time.**

**I'm in a full-out**
**LEAP OF FAITH,**
**A TRUST FALL with Spirit...**

I booked an appointment with Anthony, a local psychic medium I had a good feeling about. I thought a reading would be fun, educational and, frankly, comforting; maybe I would even do the same in other towns moving forward.

Anthony brought forward the psychic spirit guide I'd been connecting with lately, as well as my great-grandmother, who I believe was also an intuitive. I received lots of confirmation about my journey, everything I'd been receiving and doing, and allowing things to unfold. TRUST and BELIEVE were the key words that kept coming up, same as my repeated messages from earlier this morning.

Afterward, armed with a large hot, yummy latte, I went for a drive on the beautiful Blue Ridge Parkway and was able to catch some gorgeous views and end-of-day lighting. It began to snow a bit, but with the sun still shining, it was magical!

## DAY FOUR

At 6:30 a.m. I woke to the sound of my phone alarm and the cawing of crows outside. They reminded me of a conversation with Michael, when he told me he always had crows in his yard – funny, because his neighbors already thought of him as the crazy psychic with two pet wolves. That very morning I'd had my own unusual crow visitation. They usually flew outside the office window at the Raleigh house, but that day they'd all landed on the driveway where I could see them. Now, listening to them outside, I figured I had become the "crazy psychic!"

### AFTERNOON MEDITATION

Before my last two work meetings of day I sat in meditation. I always noticed such a huge difference in my connection with my clients if I took the time to meditate or attune myself beforehand. I had always kept a very clear separation between the two worlds I lived in and experienced. There was normal and metaphysical, professional and personal. It wasn't until my late thirties that I even contemplated the possibility of somehow bridging these together through mindfulness and meditation which I had begun teaching to clients and students, as well as training other clinicians to do so. These practices were still considered "woo-woo" by many, but at least they were becoming more accepted within my field as modern science and research were finally catching up with and validating these ancient traditions.

Still, when I started purposely opening up my psychic and mediumistic gifts, I never would have dreamed of going public because I was worried about how this could negatively impact my career as a clinician. The truth was that I used my psychic gifts whenever I conducted therapy sessions or attended meetings. I tuned into others' perspectives, thoughts, and emotions and would intuitively know how they would most likely respond to various scenarios. This allowed me to lead and teach in a much more effective way that would offer the most positive results for everyone involved. I would set an intention before therapy sessions and meetings and focus my energy to this end. It worked every time!

I had to be very aware of what energy I was bringing to any session or meeting and manage this beforehand, especially with my clients with autism who, though non-verbal, were highly sensitive beings. I remember the teachers of the autism classes commenting that whenever I arrived, the students would light up as if a rock-star had just entered the room. I always thought that was so funny and sweet. No wonder I fell in love with this population while still in grad school. They were sensitives like me! These special souls tended to speak with and respond to vibration much more than words. This type of non-verbal communication isn't limited to this population – we all do it, all the time – but it's definitely heightened in them. This meant I always saw my own energy reflected right back at me during sessions. The more I deepened my practice to consciously open up and hone my own psychic gifts, the more I would find myself inspired to the right activities, lessons, and words to use with them. I was in the flow and basically channeling information that would be most beneficial for any particular session or meeting.

Now, in this meditation, I was met by my spirit guides, who told me to:

*"Let go of worry you've taken on from other people.
Use this time to focus on pampering and caring for yourself.
Trust that everything you've felt and experienced is real
and allow it to unfold in time."*

I'd been having conversations with my higher self and my spirit guides for most of my life, but I always thought I was either "mental" or just plain weird and it was best to keep this under wraps. When I was alone, I would actually talk to myself aloud, asking a question and then giving myself advice!

I don't remember when this started, though I knew it was early on. Whenever I was contemplating a situation, I would find myself speaking out loud to identify the problem scenario; then, I would naturally and automatically respond aloud in the third person, "If I were you, I would..." and proceed to give myself the best solution.

Afterward, I would laugh at the lunacy of this, thinking, "If *you* were *me*?! You ARE ME!" Yet, I knew I was talking about myself, to myself, from an outside perspective.

Sometimes, the conversation happened internally, with a voice heard in my head. Other times, I would receive information and guidance through my other senses without the voice; it was more of a "thought" or download" or feeling that would let me know how to navigate a situation. My clairsentience and kinesthetic movement, which also falls under the umbrella of clairsentience, was developed early on and to a very high degree. Since I play piano, I was a naturally fast typist, and my guides and higher self utilized this skill to give me messages. In my early teens, when I was in a daydream or relaxed state, my fingers would repeatedly type words in the air until I realized what I was doing and what word or phrase was coming through to guide me.

Now, I was being guided to trust that I was connecting with Spirit and that our conversations were real. Our minds play such tricks on us and make us question everything. When we're young, we're taught that anything we sense outside of the normal 3D world isn't real, which had blocked me from opening up my gifts in the past. I have to say, it always feels good to connect with other psychics and mediums to reaffirm what I've been experiencing.

## DAY SEVEN

### Clarksville, TN

Today, I hit the road, heading west toward Clarksville, about an hour outside Nashville. On the way, I saw a truck with a huge picture of an angel and the words "Unique Transport," which let me know I was surrounded by my guides and angels.

There were some spots of traffic and some rain, but overall it was smooth, safe travels. The scenery was simply magical as I left Asheville, with the mountains partially obscured by a mist of clouds. The sun, hiding just behind them, held off the rain. The curvy roads through the mountains were fun to navigate, and I enjoyed blasting my playlists while swaying and singing the entire way. It felt so good to have some lightness and fun amidst the stormy emotions I'd been going through the past week.

After hitting some rain, I remembered to ask the Elementals and Earth Energy spirits, as well as my guides and angels, to clear the weather so I could have an easy drive. Asked and received… sunny, beautiful skies!

I didn't realize the effect I had on nature and the connection I had to the Elements and Elementals until much later in life. I remember always taking such pleasure in running or hiking and communing with nature and would do so regularly. However, I recall once being told by a fellow medium that my Korean great-grandmother had this connection and the ability to affect the weather as well.

The first time I experienced this for myself was when I was on a hike along a wooded trail in Raleigh. It was partly cloudy, but didn't look like it was going to rain so I decided to chance it and still go for a walk. Well, halfway down the trail, it didn't just start to rain, it came down in buckets! I tried finding coverage under the trees but they didn't offer any protection from the deluge, so I had no choice but to just walk or run back. At first, I just laughed at this, saying, "It's just water, no problem." Plus, I figured the angels and guides would help out and give me a break from this. Instead, the rain only seemed to get stronger. About three-quarters of the way back, I became irritated and said aloud (since there was no one else around to hear me), "Really?! Can't you guys help me out here? I'm completely soaked and have had enough! Can you please clear this up for me?" No exaggeration - not a minute later the rain came to a halt! And, immediately I had the "thought/voice" pop into my head that said, "We were waiting for you to ask." This was immediately followed up with the understanding that "they," meaning my guides, the angels, and the Elementals, cannot interfere unless I specifically ask for their help. Ah! Thank you for this understanding and reminder! This lesson solidified my surface awareness of this principle into a knowing. You learn best from experience and I have never taken the power of my connection to nature for granted since that time. Now, whenever I go on hikes I always start out my walk by thanking and consciously connecting with Mother Earth, the Elementals, and my team of helpers.

# DAY EIGHT

## Kansas City, KS

Gaining an hour as I crossed into another time zone was nice, though I had some trouble falling asleep in the new hotel room. The more I struggled, the more my thoughts and emotions overheated.

Uh oh.

More purging and releasing was obviously needed, though at least I kept the conversation civil this time. Defiant but respectful, I started negotiating with my spirit guides, boldly requesting an emergency meeting to modify and clarify our existing "contract." I restated my requirement that if they want me to fulfill my end of the deal, I would need reciprocation, in the form of a loving, supportive, nurturing relationship, to help me along this path. I'd been giving to everyone else my whole life and it was high time this was exchanged in a more balanced way.

After expressing this, I was able to fall asleep.

Later that night, as I straddled those waking and sleeping states, I got a response from my team. I needed to be aware of my own decisions and take responsibility for what I was allowing into my life in terms of relationships. I was told to:

**Let go of the timing and be cognizant of the Balance between what I'm giving with what I'm allowing myself to Receive.**

By 5 a.m. I was at a gas station, where I filled up the tank and grabbed breakfast to go. I had dropped all annoyance and was back to feeling happy and excited about this new day. Talk about roller coaster emotions! I knew it was all due to this huge transition and part and parcel to the process. I again apologized to my spirit team for my tantrum and thanked them for helping to keep my car in good condition, even in this freezing weather, with temps below twenty degrees!

Just then, on the radio, I heard "Hold the Line," courtesy of the band Toto, circa 1978. The lyrics were a direct response to my "contract negotiations" earlier! Message received. Things don't come according to my timeline, but Spirit's.

I laughed and said aloud to my unseen messengers,

"Good one! Okay, okay, got it! I'll allow the right relationship to come to me in the perfect divine timing."

It was a long, straight road across Kansas. I stopped at a McDonald's in who-knows-what-town to use the restroom and grab a coffee. While punching in my order at the automated kiosk, I could feel all eyes on me. Nothing new. I am used to standing out like a sore thumb. A young group of kids to my left was eyeing me like I'd just arrived from another country. The elderly couple to my right flat-out stared as if I'd just de-boarded the mothership. I turned to smile at them and they politely smiled back, still staring in wonderment. I felt like an alien, but at least the natives were friendly!

Having grown up in one of the only interracial families in our community, not fitting into the norm has been a lifelong theme. In fact, much of my life had been about embracing my differences (internal and external) and learning that what makes me unique is a blessing and can be used to help others ... and myself. Just as I could never hide my mixed race and cultural heritages from both sides (and never wanted to), I was now understanding that I also needed to embrace these other aspects of myself that I can't hide ... and no longer wanted to.

After landing at the hotel, I began creating new playlists for my long drive to Boulder tomorrow. The combo of music and driving always put me in a state of receiving and allowing, and nine hours on the road would give me plenty of time for that!

I then sat for a meditation with the thought to just relax and SURRENDER. I expanded my aura and light outward and saw a golden shower of light coming to replenish and heal me. Almost immediately, I felt a connection to Spirit. There was tingling and movement on my head when I began, and near the end I felt a presence and energy on my left side. The connection was getting more undeniable and stronger.

I communicated to my Spirit Guide that I needed a change in the types of romantic relationships I was attracting. I was tired of having to beg to get my needs met. That night, I put any future relationship on the altar and surrendered it to Spirit – Source – along with any fear, loneliness, sadness, and anger, asking that they be transformed back to their purest form. I also put Jared on the altar so he would receive comfort and healing energy and move on. I asked to be surrounded and imbued with protective white healing light to empower and heal me.

Suddenly, an image of me in my mid-twenties cropped up. I'd tried pot with my boyfriend and his friends and had an awful reaction. Though my boyfriend sat comforting me as I cried, I felt alone and scared. I felt like a burden.

This movie played in my head because it was how I felt in this moment, like I was needy, asking for love, connection, nurturing and not getting those needs met. I was reminded of how often I'd felt this way in my last relationship.

Another memory came then, of myself as a young child feeling alone, sad, and afraid to ask for love, affection, safety, and nurturing – though I still tried. Later in life, this manifested as severe depression and closed me off to everyone around me. This pattern was now being revealed via these "movie replays."

I saw and felt myself closing in and wilting, like a flower dying due to lack of water, sunlight, and caring. This was followed by a scene from the movie *Amelie,* when she melted and flowed down like water because her heart was breaking – the perfect visual of how I felt in this moment.

Then, I received the following message:

***Continue to release these feelings from your past.***
***What are you doing to take care of yourself?***
***Use this time to take care of yourself.***

I was inspired to a different take on an old saying:

**TREAT YOURSELF THE WAY YOU WANT OTHERS TO TREAT YOU.**

CHAPTER TWO

# WAKE-UP CALLS

*"Mistakes are great wake-up calls in that they provide you with opportunities to discover your weaknesses, what needs to be changed, and which areas of your life need improving... they can be blessings in disguise."*

**~ by John Holland**
**The Psychic Tarot Oracle Deck**

# DAY NINE

## Boulder, CO

I got another early start this morning – up at 5 a.m., excited to continue my adventure.

It was freezing cold out, but as I got on the road around seven the light was just starting in the sky and I was able to witness a beautiful sunrise. It just happened to be perfectly synced with an old favorite song, "Angel of the Morning," which played on the stereo as I entered the highway. I had the sunrise behind me as I left Kansas City and headed on the long drive to Boulder. The next song that popped up was One Republic's "Good Life," which for years had been a calling card from Spirit telling me I was plugged in and on track. I looked at my phone, which displayed the album's cool, paint-splashed cover art I had never seen before, and realized with a start that it was called *Waking Up*. Exactly how I felt!

This trip, this whole life change, was all about "waking up" to who I truly am and the life path I'm supposed to be on.

I arrived early in Boulder, enjoying the spectacular view of the Rocky Mountains surrounding the city. My new rental was just what I'd hoped for: remote, quiet, and surrounded by nature, but not far from town ... and spacious. Rather than trying to power through a hike, I just grabbed groceries, unpacked, showered, and did my meditation. Before I could blink it was 6 p.m., and I felt really good to be settled in.

When on the road that morning, I had gotten a voicemail from Jared asking if he could see me. I immediately sent out a psychic SOS to my guides and his loved ones in spirit to please surround him with healing, love, and support, and to help him move on and understand that I wasn't going to come back; that I couldn't. The last thing I wanted was for him to be hurting, but I was so ready for this leap toward this next chapter of my life. That required me to devote all my time and energy to gaining a better knowing of myself and my soul's purpose, and to expanding my psychic gifts.

With all the changes happening lately, nothing felt as complete or satisfying as sitting in meditation. That afternoon, I asked my spirit guides to come close and immediately saw the beautiful face of my main psychic guide. She said my work right now was to focus on my connection to Spirit, maintain this focus more, and **TRUST EVERYTHING THAT I'M RECEIVING** – including my connection and communication with her. She said to focus right now on healing, art, self-care, and my psychic and mediumship practice, which she would continue to help me with. It was a time for me to rebalance and attune my whole self – physically, mentally, emotionally, and spiritually. I felt so confident in my connection with her; I was also feeling the merging of this inner knowing from my soul and more trust in this future vision that was beginning to unfold before me.

## WAKE-UP CALLS

That night, I watched a video of psychic medium and spiritual teacher John Holland and Paul Selig, a psychic and an incredible channel for a spirit collective he refers to simply as "The Guides." They were speaking about accessing your higher wisdom, and John mentioned "wake-up calls" that happen in life. I was all too aware of those! At one point I was inspired to draw a card from the Psychic Tarot via my phone app (perfect for travel). The Power or Strength Card appeared before me. Note the wording on the card:

*"Mistakes are great WAKE-UP CALLS in that they provide you with opportunities to discover what needs to be changed."*

While listening I was multitasking, going about my nightly bedtime ritual. I stepped into the bathroom to grab my night cream, and when I returned to the room, the video had actually rewound to the same spot I'd heard when I left! Apparently Spirit wanted to make sure I didn't miss this message. I love the magic in synchronicities, which are happening all the time. We must simply pay attention to them.

Now that they had my full attention, I tuned in carefully to this part of the video. I was in full resonance with Paul's story about having a major kundalini awakening, which was exactly what I'd experienced several years earlier. It had led me to begin teaching meditation, and blew the door to my dormant psychic and mediumistic gifts wide open. Paul said that his Guides aren't concerned with whether people connect with or know their own guides in general, but rather that they develop their claircognizance (clear knowing). I believe this is how I've received info my whole life.

So far, this journey had allowed me the space and time for healing and introspection, and to go deeper into my connection to my own higher wisdom. Additionally, it allowed me to feel safe in exploring, expanding, and better understanding the unique gifts I have and how I can best utilize them.

As I paused the video for the night, I thought of the mediumship reading Anthony had given me in Asheville – specifically including his statement that I have gifts for platform mediumship and physical mediumship. The truth was, I had experienced both already, though in my earlier years I had tried forgetting or blocking any physical interactions with Spirit. Now, several examples of these phenomena came to mind, and I could tell I was being guided to understand and release any fear I'd had around Spirit interactions.

I recalled an occasion when I, then a young adult, didn't want my picture taken. Someone tried to take it anyway, and when we got back the developed photos I was delighted to see that a blob of light had blocked my image out completely.

At my old townhouse, my computer used to turn itself on at night. Once, I was awakened from sleep to hear a voice booming from downstairs. At first, I was frightened, but when I summoned the courage to check it out I saw that it was an inspirational video! I felt a little better, though I still didn't appreciate the timing of Spirit's playfulness. They did get my attention, though!

At my last house in North Carolina, the basement TV would turn itself on at night. The first time this happened, I was home alone and woke to the amped-up volume around midnight. It was so loud I could hear it from the third floor of the house, and I was so frightened of running into uninvited spirits that I didn't go down to turn it off until morning. After that, I always turned the volume all the way down and moved the remote away, figuring I'd make it a little bit more challenging for Spirit to mess with the electronics. Still, there were many other nights when the TV turned on, and I finally decided enough was enough. I had a stern but polite conversation with the spirits there, saying I did not want any more of these "wake-up calls" and we needed to establish some reasonable boundaries. Thank goodness it worked and they were polite enough to respect my request!

On another occasion, I was actually in the basement, having fallen asleep on the couch. In the middle of the night I woke abruptly to the sound of a group of children right outside, laughing and loudly banging on the sliding glass doors. The basement wall to the outside was basically all glass sliding doors with no curtains, so anyone on the deck would have a clear view inside. Again, I was afraid and had to muster up the courage to take a peek, only to realize that no one was physically there. The fact that these were "spiritual pranksters" was not at all comforting!

I didn't get a sense that they meant harm, but they were not there to soothe me or give me any peace and quiet either. I hightailed it upstairs as quickly as my legs would take me, hoping they wouldn't follow. Clearly, I needed to find a better way to handle my ability to see, hear, and sense spirits without freaking out every time, or hiding under the covers, as I had in the past. The next morning, I initiated a conversation with the spirits I'd been encountering in the house, telling them aloud that I did not appreciate their jokes.

"If you want to interact with me," I said, "you can do so in a more appropriate way. No more sneaking up on me and purposely scaring me. When I turn out the lights at night, I'm off duty! You can meet with me in my dreams or in the daylight. Not in the basement in the dark and, for God's sake, never in the shower!"

As crazy it sounds, it worked! I never had another episode like that again. It taught me that communication with people in the Spirit world is not so different from communication with those in the physical. I get to set the boundaries with the spirit realm regarding what I will and won't allow. I hold the power of what I experience here.

# DAY TEN

## FUCKING FAIRY DUST

The next morning, after finishing my meditation, I resumed the video from the night before and sat listening to Paul Selig channel while I had my coffee and breakfast muffin. Paul's workshops are always a combination of collective channelings from the Guides and messages for individual audience members. I was fascinated by how quickly he could remotely tap into a person on behalf of an audience member. How fun it would be, I thought, to get a reading from him! When I looked on his website, I saw that he was booked for the next 2 years! Okay, maybe not. Then I was guided to click on his upcoming events and, lo and behold, he was going to be in Denver in two days! I immediately purchased a ticket. There was obviously something for me to gain since I'd been so beautifully guided to this event, and I was prepared to see where it would lead me.

I sure do love these moments of pure magic. It was very similar to when I booked the reading with Michael: I had heard his voice in an interview and was guided to his website. That time, however, I held off, not feeling it was necessarily the right fit for me. Then I started seeing his face pop up during my meditations. After this happened repeatedly over a few weeks, I went back to his website and requested a reading. He responded quickly and we set a date and time. Somehow, my gut told me that whatever he said would be accurate and I could TRUST IT, which I'd never felt with any other previous reading. Later, he told me that he turns away nine out of ten people who ask him for a reading! Obviously this was divinely orchestrated and a big sprinkling of "fucking fairy dust," as Michael would say.

**Nothing is ever a coincidence.**
**It's all DIVINE GUIDANCE.**

***Listen to that small still voice***
***It's subtle***
***It's a quiet nudge, a thought, an inspiration***
***Don't ignore it***
***Follow it***
***It'll take you to everything you want***
***One step at a time***

***Allow the unfolding to happen in the perfect timing***
***Allow the flower to open in its own time***

*It may seem slow at times*
*It's like a beautiful symphony*
*Like divinely inspired music*
*Changing tempos*
*Like the genius comedian who plays his audience and guides them to each laugh.*

## DAY TWELVE

Talk about a wake-up call! This morning, I woke up to snow even though it's late March. Can you tell I'm not from here?

I was a bit nervous that it may make any upcoming travel difficult, but I just put it out of my mind and went about my usual routine filled with therapy sessions, two welcomed cancellations, and a great mediumship group during which I was gifted with a beautiful and emotional reading for my sitter, Danielle.

Oftentimes, people come to a mediumship reading wanting or demanding to hear from a particular loved one in spirit. However, whoever comes through is up to the Spirit world; the medium does not "summon" anyone. Sometimes, spirits will come in together, with one communicating first as if leading the way for another.

This is what happened with Danielle. A more senior family member stepped forward first, followed by her daughter. The young woman was a great communicator, offering clear evidence of her identity. But when I clairvoyantly saw the symbol of a butterfly, Danielle had no shadow of a doubt that her daughter was here with us; it was the symbol she associated most with her beloved daughter, representing her transition and transformation in the afterlife. The daughter then showed herself to me shifting into this beautiful glowing angel, telling me that she now served as her mom's guardian – something Danielle definitely felt in her heart to be true.

It was a lovely reading, making both her mom and me well up with emotion. But the best part was afterward, when Danielle shared that she had secretly hoped and wished for her daughter to come through since she doesn't usually! Truly, our spirit people are always by our side, knowing what we need most and always offering their love and support.

This is exactly why I do this sacred work...
to be able to offer this kind of healing
and connection.

# DAY THIRTEEN

### Moab, Utah

This morning, I woke before my alarm, excited to get on the road. First things first, though; I did my meditation, then sat with a cup of coffee, thinking of the Paul Selig workshop I had attended the night before. He led us through an exercise in which we connected to the person beside us and "attuned" them to the energy The Guides were sharing. I worked with Shondra, who had arrived just at the last minute and sat down next to me.

We were asked to turn toward our partner and stare into their eyes, which is very difficult and uncomfortable for most people. I didn't just see Shondra's physical form in front of me, I saw her soul. I could see her as pure golden light and energy, the Divine spark. When someone sees you, really sees into you like this, it can be very emotional. I felt pure bliss and Shondra was brought to tears.

During the event, I thought about how I had gotten the opportunity to get a reading from Paul after all – it seemed like he kept looking right at me, waiting for me to raise my hand. However, what came to mind whenever I thought about it was a certain knowing, which came to me this morning in the following download:

*You already have the knowledge and the answers you need right now. There is such freedom in the lesson of trusting and surrendering, not needing to know the final destination or even the next thing just yet. All will be revealed in the perfect timing one step at a time, as it always has.*

*Take a chance and then just pivot as needed. Don't NOT make a move because you're scared to make the wrong move. Maybe it's good to start making more wrong moves or taking more gambles!*

*If you are not making mistakes or experiencing some missteps along the way, you probably aren't taking big enough risks. You're probably playing it too safe and not experimenting or playing enough in the process. How can you step out and take a bigger risk, which will inevitably lead to growth and bigger changes in the evolution of your soul?*

In other words, there wasn't anything that Paul needed to tell me that I didn't already know. I knew what I needed to know for now. And anything I didn't know yet would be revealed in the right time. There's really no fun in knowing everything or always having someone give me the answers. I was guided to have more trust and surrender in the unfolding... being ok with the NOT KNOWING. Even being OK with possibly making a misstep or "mistake" because there's so much value even in that. No longer relying on those outside of myself for the answers. No longer allowing what other people tell me to take precedence over my own inner guidance. I was being told to:

**TRUST IN MY OWN ABILITY TO FIND THE WAY.**

I thought about an episode of Jerry Seinfeld's *Comedians in Cars Getting Coffee.* Jerry describes a scene from an old movie where a dad in a station wagon is stopped at a light and a guy on a motorcycle rolls up next to him. The dad in the car appears in awe of him, sitting on that bike with complete freedom and adventure in front of him.

Most people would never do what I'm doing now. Some wouldn't want to, while others wouldn't or couldn't for a variety of reasons. All I know is, I feel like that guy on the motorcycle right now, wild and free, and I thank God for it!

The drive to Moab took me through Vail, Colorado and its famous ski areas, which was beautiful but also stressful because of the snowy and icy roads. My concerns about the route I had taken and how my car would hold up turned out to be unfounded. I asked for the Spirit world for protection, safe passage, and clear weather, and they came through as always.

There was a short distance between the sign announcing you have left Colorado and the one welcoming you to Utah. As I drove through this area, I was reminded of the concept of liminal space, something I often teach about. This was where I currently found myself – having left the past behind without knowing what would be on the other side of this adventure. Just trusting that all would work out and that the next step would be revealed when it needed to be.

My work in the meantime was to allow the changes to come;
tune myself to a higher vibration;
improve my ability to maintain my focused energy
at this higher level;
to be open and receptive to the guidance and influence
of the Spirit world;
to remember who I am and allow myself to step
into my power, and to

**SURRENDER TO MY TRUE PATH.**

Crossing into Utah was nothing short of magical! I had left the dark clouds threatening rain and snow behind me in Colorado and was now headed toward a sunny, clear, expansive sky with fluffy white clouds floating across it. This was the perfect analogy for my journey, and confirmation from Spirit that the life I was stepping into would be a stark contrast from the past.

No wonder I was guided to make a stop in Moab! It was gorgeous, surrounded by huge, snowcapped mountains in the distance and amazing red rock formations everywhere. Arriving at the hotel, I was exhausted from the stress of the drive but so happy to have landed in this stunning landscape.

Almost as soon as I closed my eyes for my meditation, I felt plugged in, in a very strong way. I felt twitches and tingles throughout my body, a sign that Spirit has drawn near.

My guide appeared, looking like an angel – white, glowing, and almost floating in front of me. It was different from the way I usually experienced her. It felt more real, alive, visceral.

She shared that though my guides had tried to steer me on my spiritual path much earlier in life, I still had to go through some "normal" human experiences too.

She said not to worry about the past or the timing. What matters is where I'm at NOW and where I'm going in my future. I'm on track and exactly where I need to be. In fact, she praised me for the bravery of having taken such swift action forward on my path.

I felt her with me while driving into Utah on the long, beautiful road, with the sun in the sky, windows open for some fresh air, music blasting, and me feeling exhilaration for this feeling of pure freedom. I could sense her laughing and cheering with me – reveling in my enjoyment of life!

# DAY FOURTEEN

*"Remembering the story of your own life helps you open up more and allows you to 'come out' as a psychic medium. This was always your trajectory and always your path."*

**~Pam Meredith**

Woke up around 3 a.m. to downloads flooding in with insights on some major hardships in my life and why I went through them. I felt called to journal them, and just as I was writing about the repeated pattern I'd experienced in my relationship with Jared, the journal shut down and erased it!! Hmmm, interesting. Perhaps it's a sign that *it's time to put that pattern to rest.* Across our tumultuous relationship, I had attracted the same erratic behavior from him that I'd experienced throughout my childhood with my mother. Underlying their volatility was a feeling of fear and overwhelm. They were unable to care, nurture, and give love openly and unconditionally to me because they could barely handle the inner and outer turmoil happening for themselves.

I also wrote about a very traumatic event that happened when I was around six years old. As mentioned earlier, my dad, who served in the Army, was shipped off to Korea for a "hardship tour," leaving me, my mom, and my sister behind in the States for a whole year. During that time, my poor Korean mom was trying her best to take care of us while struggling to master English and with no one to turn to for support. Worse still, his absence left us vulnerable to a racist element in our community, who targeted us for a hate crime.

Knowing that Dad wasn't around to protect her, some neighbors who lived down the street from us physically assaulted my mom right on our property. They were making fun of her for not being able to speak English fluently and for being Asian. Completely unconcerned that other neighbors could witness their attack, they held her down and threatened to stab her with a pair of scissors while another neighbor held me and my sister back. Luckily someone called the police to come help. I remember all of us crying afterward, distraught as we tried to figure out how and why this happened. I recall blaming myself for somehow causing it, and for a long time I felt guilty and terrified about not being able to protect or help my mom.

This and other early childhood experiences had created fear-based survival patterns of people-pleasing and wanting to blend in for fear of drawing negative backlash. No wonder, considering how I had seen first-hand what could happen to those who are "different"!

I also traced this to a recurring nightmare I had, throughout my childhood and even into my adult life, in which people were trying to break into our home through the back entry sliding glass doors. In the dream, I was always trying, unsuccessfully, to close and lock them, and for many years the invaders would be able to get inside and attack me. Thankfully, as my lucid dreaming skills developed in my teen years, I began to take back my power and stop their physical attack, though I still could never seem to lock those damn doors!

As crazy as it may sound, I was able to look back and find a silver lining in those dramatic events of my childhood – they made me a much stronger, more resilient person. It's my belief that my earlier years were designed to empower me to remember my own self-worth, embrace my differences, and realize that my freedom comes from within.

I'm understanding more and more that regardless of what others are telling me or what I'm experiencing around me, the things that make me unique are a strength and I do not need external approval, love, or validation. This was a lesson I had to live in order to know and trust it within myself. Furthermore, it forced me to develop and heighten my natural intuition and ability to read others as a matter of self-preservation and survival. Trauma often makes you dissociate from this limited physical reality as a survival mechanism. In fact, I've heard it said that most mediums have experienced some kind of trauma in their lives.

Looking back at these experiences, I could actually muster a sense of compassion and understanding for the people in these recollections. But I followed that up with the affirmation that I was done putting up with anyone else's bullshit or mistreatment. I'd allowed this to happen way too many times, but no more.

I would only accept relationships where I was respected, loved unconditionally, heard, appreciated ... no longer bullied or taken for granted. I intended to be able to express myself honestly without worry of judgment, punishment, or backlash. I finally felt SAFE and FREE here on my own and I didn't have to worry about the needs or wants of other people.

CHAPTER THREE

# NEW BEGINNINGS

*"Most people are afraid of change and play it safe by staying where they are. Know that through inner guidance, wisdom, and a belief in yourself you'll be propelled forward on a positive, life-changing path. Don't conform to what society or other individuals expect of you at this time. It's your own adventure."*

**~ by John Holland**
**The Psychic Tarot Oracle Deck**

# DAY FIFTEEN

## Phoenix, AZ

The drive out of Moab was beautiful, though there was snow all around. Crossing the border into Arizona was clearly delineated as the landscape transitioned to less and less snow, with patches of brown and red clay, and finally, the mountains and saguaro cacti of Phoenix, Valley of the Sun.

When I arrived at my rental, I jumped right into work mode: unpacked, grabbed some groceries, washed my car that was covered with dirt and snow-melting salt, started a load of laundry and then savored a nice hot shower. Funny, though, how once I was physically settled in, a stream of troublesome emotions began to emerge. I felt scared, unclear, and unsupported. I felt like I didn't belong here. I had begun this adventure assuming that I might start to feel "at home" in some of these places I was drawn to visit and that I might even find a place I could plant roots in the near future. However, I had not felt at home in Asheville, the Nashville area, Boulder, Moab, and not here in Phoenix either. I needed connection, comfort, grounding, peace of mind, community, and love, but I didn't have anyone here in the physical to offer this to me.

I immediately sat for a meditation to ground myself. I communicated to Spirit that although I loved our connection and the freedom of following my spiritual path, I needed to be able to experience loving physical human relationships too. I needed a romantic partner who can give me comfort, love, support, and a place to call home. Don't get me wrong, I love to travel and this is very important to me. However, I also longed to one day find a place and a person I can call home.

In fact, being on the road had little to do with why I was feeling this way, though it did bring it to the fore. I had never really felt at home or like I belonged, even with my own family and certainly not in any of my romantic relationships. Living with Jared the last few years, I always felt like an unwelcome guest who could be kicked out at any time. I can't tell you how many times I had a bag packed or back-up plan about what I would do and where I could possibly go, just in case.

I told the Spirit world and Source that I was surrendering to them, to this path, and to my true soul purpose. That's why I had given up everything and was here in this unknown place. I was literally and figuratively making movement in my life, just as they wanted. But I also needed for them to show me some movement on their end.

During my meditation, in which I called in the whole team to help comfort me, heal me, and guide me, I immediately felt a connection to energy. I could viscerally feel and see energy moving around and through my body and knew the angels, healers, helpers, and guides were attuning me and ramping up the healing to clear all of this worrisome anxious energy and put me at ease. I sensed my clairaudience turning on and I could hear the soft sound of angelic music.

A little bit later, I pulled a Psychic Tarot card for myself and received "NEW BEGINNINGS," which calls forth one's inner courage as they take that leap of faith and step into the unknown.

**"Through inner guidance, wisdom, and a belief in yourself (and tapping into these tools) you'll be propelled forward on a positive life changing path. Give yourself permission to live, play, love, and, above all, laugh."**

I received the following downloads from my team to give me further guidance in reference to this card and its message for me:

**FACE YOUR FEARS**
***so that new people and***
***conditions can manifest.***
***Yes, you may feel fear,***
***but still moving forward anyway.***
***You're forgetting how strong you really are!***
***Do anything that will remind you how strong you are.***
***Make it your daily mantra to remind yourself that***
***YOU POSSESS ALL THE TOOLS INSIDE OF YOU!***

## DAY SIXTEEN

This morning while drinking coffee, I was greeted by several doves flying by my window. One would stop just over my window and would hang upside down to look at me. It did this several times. I love when birds act silly around me. Over the years, Spirit has tended to work through birds and other animals to watch me or give me signs that they're around.

It reminded me of my sweet, persistent cardinal that visited me almost daily for months at my last home. And it didn't just look for me in one window, but began searching for me in other windows around the house, too. Oftentimes, I would wake to the sound of it trying to get inside, all the while looking for me, as if letting me know it was time to get up for my morning meditation.

Now, another bird lightly bumped itself against the window, trying to get inside, and then flew off. Then a dove flew over and actually hovered for a moment right in front of my window like a hummingbird, trying to look inside at me, just like my cardinal used to do. I loved and appreciated these signs from Spirit that they were watching over me here, too.

## DAY SEVENTEEN

While eating breakfast, I was entertained once again by the dove hanging upside down from the rooftop to peek inside at me. It then flew back and landed on the ground, walking back and forth trying to see me inside. Finally, it flew up and hovered in front of the window again!

I hiked my new favorite trail for the second time and had lots of inspired thoughts coming through, including mantras like, **"I TRUST THAT EACH STEP WILL BE GUIDED AND SUPPORTED."** As I looked in front of me to be guided to the next best step, I thanked the rocks beneath me, each grain of sand, and each plant, seeing each as interconnected and all playing a part in creating this solid foundation that was supporting me on my journey. I could almost feel an invitation from particular rocks to "step here" for a stable place to land.

As I passed these bright yellow flowers, it reminded me of my mom saying that flowers sometimes looked like they're smiling at us. I'd always found being in nature so healing, and now I literally felt at one with nature. Yet, I also felt tired, unlike yesterday when I had an abundance of energy. Today was a day to move slowly and just take it easy. No need to hurry.

**Savor and enjoy the path**
**be okay with things coming in their own time**
**Not forcing, but allowing**
**Not requiring the details of when or how**
**Letting it unfold like a flower**
**Letting it be revealed to me.**

I had an incoming call from a friend, which was nice, but I just didn't feel like talking to anyone. It was a push and pull of wanting connection but simultaneously wanting time alone and really needing some solitude to be left to my own thoughts.

It reminded of how a few years back I had considered joining a monastery, or at least going off on a solo journey as I was doing now. Instead, I had made the conscious choice to not only remain in society, but to move in with Jared and give our relationship a real shot. Both were needs I had – had I been postponing my purpose or was this a divinely guided detour because Spirit knew I had more to learn from that situation?

I was also thinking about how challenging it can sometimes be to trust because I'd been betrayed or hurt in the past. Yet I kept making the choice every day to open my heart more, give and receive love, and move toward a place of increased trust.

During my morning meditation I had a vision in which I transformed into a fiery phoenix. It was a perfect symbol, not only because I was physically here in Phoenix, but also because of this new beginning I was moving into. In the vision, I began to strip off my outer physical layers to reveal my inner light and power. Then I flew upward, leaving all the old layers behind.

ANOTHER HELPFUL MANTRA:

**Every day I'm shedding another layer and stepping more into my true power and gifts.**

## DAY TWENTY

It was my regular routine – waking five minutes before my alarm and meditating, followed by coffee and breakfast.

I thought about how disciplined my routine was and how that really accounted for the way my skills had unfolded. This was something I learned at a young age, when I was taking piano lessons and had to be disciplined in order to see results. Classically trained, my sister and I both started at five years old and were required by our parents to practice for one hour each day. Even "on vacation" – when we went to visit our grandma in El Paso – we had to practice on her electric keyboard. It was actually kinda fun to play Mozart with a rhumba beat behind it. I think he would have gotten a kick out of this modern-day harpsichord!

Some people think of discipline as a "four-letter" word; for me, setting the alarm and carving out designated, non-negotiable time to meditate every single day is essential for developing a more intimate relationship with Spirit. It shows the Spirit world that you are putting forth the deliberate intention to connect and that this is important to you. As with any skill, you have to deliberately work to develop your abilities, regardless of your natural talents, in order to see them flourish and expand. Even the Buddha didn't stop meditating after his enlightenment. A daily meditation practice improves your ability to maintain focus, recalibrates you to a higher vibration, increases your intuitive sensitivity, and strengthens your spiritual muscles. Plus, it happens to be my absolute favorite time of the day. The hard part is coming back into my physical body!

## DAY TWENTY-TWO

Today I packed up all my stuff in preparation of the move to another rental for my next week in Phoenix. I arrived early to the Abraham Hicks event so I could reserve a seat up front. Then I wandered to a quiet place in an upstairs lobby of the hotel as I was highly inspired to do some writing.

This morning, I was thinking a lot about CHOICE vs DESTINY. What came to me was that DESTINY is what comes about through the incremental choices and preferences we've made along our path. We are called to our destiny and what we most want, even when we don't fully realize it in the moment or think that we are co-creating. This is not just about wanting to do something, but having to do it because it's a soul calling.

In other words, Destiny and Choice are really two sides of the same coin.

Your destiny is the accumulation and result of what YOU have chosen for yourself each step of the way, while incorporating the plan you made before coming to Earth for this incarnation. The plan is not set in stone; it's mutable and changes based on the evolving preferences and choices you create through experiencing life – and, yet, the big picture largely remains constant. That feeling or pull toward something, the desire to move in a particular direction, is guided by your Higher Self and your team of helpers who are always able to see the bigger picture. At the same time, you are part of the co-creative process, making choices on your own – and taking risks as well.

It seems that oftentimes people don't want to take ownership over their own role in the creation of their lives. They have also become addicted to instant gratification and expect immediate manifestation instead of allowing the process of creation to unfold. No surprise there – we live in an age when we click a button and an Amazon Prime truck driver shows up, same day, with the product we need and/or desire. An electronic download is even quicker; in fact, waiting thirty seconds for something to load on our phone feels unacceptable and often leads to frustration bordering on outrage. The thing is, the Universe doesn't work quite like Amazon; it takes intention and discipline to become attuned and aware of your intuitive guidance, as well as the focused energy to then take the inspired action. It also takes courage to know that some of your attempts won't work out. It takes wisdom to understand that, in reality, it's always working out – even those things that seem like mistakes or errors. And, finally, it takes fortitude and tenacity to repeat this again and again each new day.

People often confuse their need to make things happen – in the way they want it to happen – with inspiration from Spirit or from their Higher Self. Other times, they might be aware of an inspiration but just aren't ready for it yet. For example, I always felt a calling toward alternative healing work, but I didn't act on it until now. I'd also known for many years that my relationship with Jared wasn't right, but I just wasn't ready to let it go. Then, one day, I had the *knowing* in my heart and in my gut that it was time. The more you practice tapping in and honing your sensitivity and ability to interpret your guidance, the better you'll get at discerning the difference between your Higher Self, that's guiding you with wisdom, and your ego self, that's trying to keep you small, stuck, and "safe."

When you begin to meditate, you learn to relax your body and quiet your mind, which is the prerequisite to being able to tap into and sense that there is more to YOU and to this life than the matrix of the physical experience you can see/feel/touch. For the small portion of the population who maintains a meditation practice, it will indeed be only "practice," because they are so caught up in their logical mind and their daily thoughts, stresses, and worries. I often hear from people, "I can't meditate, I can't quiet my mind, my mind is too busy." And, *so it is,* because they have called it into being with their words.

Those who can relax their body and mind enough to open up to the next layer will begin to build a relationship with themselves – with their Higher Selves, their spirit selves. It takes time, and a relatively small number of individuals will entertain that this relationship and experience is possible, but I believe this number is growing.

If you can get to this place of possibility, you can begin to cultivate your inner power and eventually KNOW the Divine Energy and Source that dwells inside of you. You will start to open your awareness to the non-physical reality (which is actually here in plain sight) if you allow yourself to see/feel/sense through a different lens. Now, after having been a meditator and on my spiritual path for most of my life, whenever I close my eyes with the intention to connect with my spirit team, it happens in an instant. They're always here with me, and the fact that I acknowledge them and deliberately intend to blend, connect, commune, and clearly communicate makes it much more visceral.

Now, I was in a time of ALLOWING, SURRENDERING, TRUSTING. I'd put a whole lot into my "vortex" – Abraham Hicks' word for the pure positive vibrational holding tank for all our desires for our lives – and my "work" was to TRUST AND ALLOW it to come. However, that doesn't mean stopping my daily meditations or following through with inspired action, like attending my weekly psychic and mediumship circles, et cetera. I just don't need to have so much of the angst, worry or battle over things that haven't manifested yet. There will always be something in the pot that is in a state of becoming so I might as well enjoy the process, the journey.

***"Don't go looking for your path. Prepare yourself vibrationally so it appears beneath your feet."***

**~ Abraham-Hicks**

CHAPTER FOUR

# AWARENESS

***"You already possess all of the tools to guide and direct you in your life. Once you learn to tap into and use them, you'll be amazed by the power and effect they can have."***

**~ by John Holland**
**The Psychic Tarot Oracle Deck**

# DAY TWENTY-FOUR

### The Soul's Path

***It's the path that may not make sense to anyone,***
***even you,***
***yet your heart and soul are still calling you that way.***
***Remember that it's okay to be scared, but then do it anyway.***
***You will be supported, guided, and rewarded.***
***Follow your soul's path;***
***It'll lead you to everything you want, your destiny,***
***and your true self.***

I had a few minutes to spare before my first therapy session, so I did a quick check-in, pulling one tarot card. It was the same card that had come up for me yesterday: AWARENESS. It was a very positive card and, I'd heard it said that it "is often drawn when you're ready to switch direction … or change careers." It spoke to me about the opening of my psychic abilities now more than ever.

In the afternoon, wanting to soak up some fresh air and sunshine, I went for a nice hike on the trail, moving slowly up and down. Whenever I had the smallest subtle urge to take a picture, I did. I didn't take any communication or inspiration for granted any more. As I hiked, I listened to a new song, shared by my mentor today, that brought me to tears. The singer's sweet voice, the gentle melody, and the lyrics about patience and manifesting a dream, deeply resonated with me.

On the way down, I took my time, taking careful steps and stopping to appreciate the beautiful plants, rocks, trees. There was a man walking swiftly behind me and, rather than feeling rushed I stopped to let him pass then continued at my own pace. When I caught up to him again further down the trail, I learned he had encountered – and almost stepped on – a very poisonous rattlesnake! It was right in the middle of the trail, and its colors made it difficult to see if you weren't paying attention. He was lucky to have seen it in time and I was lucky he was ahead of me. Ah, AWARENESS! Just goes to show how we're always being guided and protected, but it's also up to us to do our part to be sensitive to the signs, and to be aware of our surroundings.

## DAY TWENTY-FIVE

Phoenix… so appropriate that I was still in this city whose name and symbolism was exactly aligned with my visions. I had continued to see myself shedding my outer physical layer, shedding past experiences and relationships, shedding the identity largely based on how others saw me and the one I'd hid behind, thus allowing my inner phoenix and fire energy to rise up and out.

### WISDOM FROM THE TRAIL

Everyone moves at a different pace and is guided to their path of least resistance based on where they're at. This is not always the quickest path. It's not always the straightest, most direct route. Sometimes we have to take a windy path that zigs and zags.

On the trail today, I moved at twice the pace as the day before. I just felt more fired up – angry and annoyed at times, but more energetic, nonetheless. The hike helped me harness and refocus that fire and transmute it into kinesthetic energy, moving me with speed up this mountain.

Along the way I received texts from Jared on what he thought I should do to move forward with my journey. I knew he was trying to be encouraging and helpful, but no one knew what I needed like I did. Honestly, I wasn't completely sure what that was, but I trusted that I was being guided to it. Like the singer I had listened to yesterday, I was just being patient as I was creating a new dream.

As I headed off the trail at the end of my hike, I was guided to look at an area of the trail to my right. There, on the ground, my eyes landed on this beautiful rock of many colors. Just the other day I'd been thinking how I wanted to find a rock from this special trail that had been so healing and comforting to me. Instead, this rock had found me and called out to me to get my attention! I picked it up and felt it vibrating in my hand, which surprised me so much that I looked down at it to see if there was something on it like a bug. Of course, there wasn't – it was definitely the rock, and I loved feeling its vibration, its energy. We forget that everything in existence is vibrating energy, including us. And that is exactly why I wanted to bring a rock with me and keep it, no matter where I go on my trip. That'll remind me of and surround me with the same healing energy I felt while walking this trail.

## DAY TWENTY-EIGHT

It was Good Friday, and my last full day in Phoenix. After an easy morning, I finished my work sessions early then did a quick, one-card pull from my tarot deck. For the third day in a row, I had received the AWARENESS card! I decided to open the guidebook and see what messages stood out to me as there was obviously something Spirit was guiding my attention to. It read:

The Traditional Tarot Archetype for the Awareness card is:

**THE MAGICIAN**

**"You have the ability to allow the Universe to work in partnership with you. Together you can manifest change... and bring about a positive outcome."**

I closed my eyes and connected with my Higher Self for any further guidance on this card, and I received this:

**SIGNS AND ENCOURAGEMENT ARE EVERYWHERE, YOU JUST HAVE TO OPEN YOUR AWARENESS TO THEM.**

Keeping that in mind, I immediately changed clothes and jumped in my car to get it checked and ready for my pending drive to my next destination: Sedona. There was a long wait at the auto shop, with a few cars already parked in front of me, but any thoughts of leaving ended when another car pulled up behind me. I had no choice now but to wait, which was fine since I wasn't in any hurry and needed to get this done.

## THE CRASH

Finally, it was my turn. The attendant was so nice, saying that even though I wasn't in their system he would still take care of me as a courtesy, free of charge. Awesome! After a quick service, I thanked the man and waved him goodbye then pulled out and stopped right by the road to find my directions to the trailhead. As I always do before pulling out, I looked carefully both right and left to watch for oncoming traffic; then, anticipating an opening soon, I took my foot off the brake, allowing the car to start gently pulling itself forward.

Suddenly, out of nowhere, a man on a bike appeared and bumped the right corner of my car, the impact causing him to tip right over onto the ground. It was as if time shifted into slow motion. My heart stopped and I had a moment of shock immediately followed by a WTF?!!

After what felt like a huge gap of time but was actually about a second, my brain signaled my arm to start working again; I put my car in park and pulled on the emergency break so I could jump out and help this poor man. Incredibly, at the same time I was doing all this, I was also watching the following sequence in absolute amazement: the man swiftly but casually stood, dusted himself off, walked over to my window, and parked his bike – all by the time I had one foot out the door. How the hell did he move so quickly?!

At my passenger window, he leaned in to check me out. As soon as we locked eyes, his initial, more serious expression transitioned to a soft, gentle one.

"Oh my goodness, sir, are you alright?!" I exclaimed.

After confirming no damage was done, he proceeded to explain that he preferred to ride against traffic; he also admitted that even though he'd clearly seen me looking the other way for oncoming cars, he made the stupid decision to try to ride out in front of me. He actually apologized to me! I profusely returned the apologies, and we agreed that we both needed to be more AWARE of our surroundings. He then put out his hand for a fist bump and I grabbed it and gave it a big squeeze with both hands, so thankful he was unharmed and for his obvious kindheartedness.

I told him to please go first and that I wouldn't move an inch until I knew he was completely out of the way. He laughed as he rode off, while I sat there, again thinking, WTF??!! Why did that just happen?? I didn't know, but it had certainly gotten all of my attention!

By the time I made it to my hiking trail, I was so ready to be out of the car and call upon my team of guides, archangels, healers, and helpers to please completely clear me of any and all negative energy that could have possibly created such a situation. As I walked listening to my music for some much-needed regrouping and healing, I sensed a quickening in the vibration around my body. I knew I was tuning into my guides as they approached to offer support and guidance.

They made me *aware* that this man had been guided into my experience as a wake-up call. Uh, well guys, it worked! In my mind's eye, I was again shown the image of the AWARENESS card I'd been drawing repeatedly for the past few days, then received the following download:

***"BE AWARE, but not afraid.***
***Realize you are always protected and supported.***
***Also, realize the magic you possess and bring forth into the world***
***to alchemize or positively influence any person or situation."***

I was then reminded of an incident that occurred when I was living in Raleigh. I'd pulled into a corner gas station and was headed for a pump when I noticed another car rolling up toward the series of open pumps just a beat behind me. When I got out of my car, I saw the other car had parked across from mine; the driver, a man, was glaring at me. He proceeded to tell me that he'd intended to take the exact pump I was parked at.

Surprised by his annoyance, I said, "I'm sorry. I didn't realize that. We both pulled up around the same time. If I'd known that, I would have gone to another pump."

I saw his whole demeanor relax as he realized that I had no selfish or malicious intent.

"Oh, it's okay, don't worry about it," he said, yet I still wondered why I had attracted that into my experience, especially since I was in a good mood! A moment later, I received an answer on the video screen by my pump.

Between ads, there it was, the "word of the day": **MOLLIFY,** which means to soothe or calm, to lessen the anger or agitation of someone! I had been gifted with the opportunity to offer calming energy to this man, who was obviously annoyed about other things happening in his life. That frustration had manifested into his outburst toward me and, through that interaction, I was able to give him a different way of looking at things that shifted him emotionally and mentally.

The man on the bike reminded me that I bring to every situation the ability to transform experiences and perspectives that may appear negative but are actually opportunities for shifting and alchemizing energy. The downloaded message continued:

> ***"You bring an energy with you to the world in which you are able to calm and transmute situations that might otherwise have been disastrous, volatile, or negative, which is needed at this time more than ever. Stay ALERT and be ready for the unexpected. Be brave, have no fear as you continue forward. Aware, but not fearful."***

Then, trying to lighten things up, my team made me aware of the scene from *ELF* when Will Ferrell's character first arrives in New York City, gets hit by a taxi while crossing the road, and immediately jumps up and says, "Sorry!" Spirit definitely has a sense of humor, I thought as I laughed aloud at this image.

I'd heard stories about angels or guides who show up in human form and wondered if the man on the bike had been one of them. Whether he was or not, I was grateful for the way the situation turned out, and I would certainly move forward with a keener awareness of the signs around me.

At the top of the mountain, I seated myself on my favorite bench to take in the gorgeous view. When I saw a couple looking toward me and pointing, I took out my earbuds and asked if I had taken their bench. I'd be happy to move if they wanted to sit down. The woman said no, they had seen me coming up the mountain and wondered if I had actually just hiked the whole trail. I confirmed that I had and she said, "Wow! You made it up so quickly! We were watching you moving."

She told me they were just visiting Phoenix for the day with their daughter, who had been born here. When they lived here she'd often hiked this trail, and the best part was making it to the top and enjoying the view. It made her so happy, she added, that her daughter was sitting on the rock, doing just that. And, she loved that she had seen me there doing the same thing. I agreed with her, saying how important it is that we take time to "SAVOR THE VIEW." So many people made it to the top and turned right back around without soaking in the moment or taking time to just appreciate the peak. Such a sweet family, and what a beautiful connection with some strangers. I certainly needed it.

I felt emotional as I descended, knowing this was the last time I'd be hiking this trail, maybe ever. I had been here almost every day over the last two weeks and it was such a healing space for me. My soul really connected to the energy, making it feel like home. As usual, I saw the faces of the flowers smiling at me, I felt the energy from the rocks and trees, and I even saw one of the trees, whose branches looked like a hand waving goodbye.

CHAPTER FIVE

# IN THE WOMB

*"Manifestation of growth is on the horizon. You're the creator and the seeds that have been planted are now ready to give birth into your world. Be patient as you watch your seeds take root and grow. Giving birth to a new creation. Cradled and held in the womb. Not yet ready for birth, but being fertilized."*

**~ by John Holland**
**The Psychic Tarot Oracle Deck**

# DAY TWENTY-NINE

## Sedona, AZ

I came out of my 5:30 a.m. meditation, which focused on opening and activating the chakras, with such a sense of groundedness and certainty that I was on the right path. I knew I was exactly where I needed to be in this moment and trusted that I was headed to the next right location as well.

I appeared to be expanding at a faster rate than most people might expect, but that was because I'd already done so much prep work across my lifetime to dive deep, better understand myself, and set the stage for everything that was manifesting now. My discipline over time was accelerating my unfoldment in the present.

Around the age of 17, I began meditating and diving deep into all things metaphysical, which, back in the early 90's, was not as readily accessible and mainstream as it is today. This was the start of my spiritual quest in which I consciously made the decision to step fully onto this path. I read and incorporated anything that had to do with self transformation and studied about all types of spirituality and religion. I had a daily practice of dreamwork including dream analysis, understanding and interpreting the language and symbolism of my dreams, and experimenting in lucid dreaming. Other daily practices included journaling, connecting with nature, and a gratitude practice. I began dabbling in astrology, numerology, tarot cards even palm reading, and would do mini readings for my family including analyzing their dreams.

I adopted a mindfulness practice in my everyday life, and was beginning to understand the law of attraction. I was becoming much more aware of my connection to everyone and everything around me and the role I played in what I experienced. I began making more conscious decisions in my words, actions, thought, and who/what I surrounded myself with.

Looking back now, I understood that I wasn't learning anything new, but was awakening to the remembrance of what I already knew. It was also at that time that I began to use the power of visualization and intention. I would project energy throughout my body and could viscerally feel and sense its movement, temperature, and color. I would surround myself in a bubble of white light to protect myself from outside energies or influences. I had felt disempowered my whole life and this was my first real experience in reclaiming my personal power.

Today in my mediumship circle, our teacher talked about how our minds love to hijack situations, and our lives, with negative self-talk. It's up to each of us to drop down, out of our mind and into our heart and center in order to hear the wisdom of our soul. It's up to us to become our own guru and stop questioning the answers that are coming in. Mediumship takes a lot of personal strength, courage, and perseverance. We have to be discerning and constantly ask ourselves, "Where are you sourcing your information?"

After class, I got the nudge to check out the website of another teacher, Caroline Cory, and saw she would be speaking in Sedona on my last day there! Thrilled, I immediately bought tickets to this event and extended my cabin rental for two more nights.

It was another example of perfect timing and synchronicity... all part of the plan. As I packed up the car and slid behind the wheel, ready to head to Sedona, I wondered what I would experience there.

## INSPIRATION ON THE ROAD

At times, my life feels like one big synchronistic event, like so much has been orchestrated for me. It's not that I'm being manipulated or that everything is preplanned; rather, it's like creating a piece of art, such as a photograph. When you start out, you have a good idea of what you want to create, but you don't really know exactly what the final product will look like until you've gone through all the processing. Sometimes you're inspired to add different colors or play with different filters as you go. The image gets tweaked; it develops and evolves and usually becomes something so much greater than you originally imagined. That's what life is like, a beautiful yin and yang of destiny and co-creation.

## THE ARTIST'S CABIN

As soon as I got to the artist's cabin (aka tiny house), I immediately felt inspired and knew it was just perfect for me. After unpacking and setting myself up, I laid down for an hour-long meditation, which helped relieve my headache.

While my dinner was in the microwave, I poured a glass of wine and searched for *Close Encounters of the Third Kind,* which had been mentioned in my mediumship group. I thought I'd seen Spielberg's science fiction classic, which is about contact with benevolent extraterrestrial beings, years before, but it all seemed new to me now. Wow, I thought, noting it had been released in 1977, the graphics had really held up!

Before bed, I was reminded of my drive here, particularly the feeling I had as I headed down that long, bumpy, dirt road to this ranch – a place I had stayed a couple of years earlier. It was more than a feeling, actually; it was a KNOWING that I was coming to the exact right place, on the exact right day. Now I reflected on the unfoldment of a series of synchronicities I had been guided through, starting with Caroline Cory's video. From there I was led to her site, where I learned she would be at a conference here in Sedona, followed by the ease with which I had extended my own stay. Finally, on the day of my arrival, I had received inspiration to watch *Close Encounters*, which came back, full circle, to Caroline Cory's videos on ETs and otherworldly encounters. I had the thought that this might sound crazy to others; to me, it was just how life rolls and I wouldn't change these kinds of seemingly magical "coincidences" for the world.

## DAY THIRTY

I usually got up around 5 a.m. But today, the first morning in my tiny Sedona home, also happened to be Easter Sunday. Knowing I'd have this whole, quiet day to myself, I just rolled over and slept in, which felt amazing. Sometimes you don't realize how tired you really are until you're given the luxury of time and space for rest. Today, I was gifting that to myself – no scheduled "have-tos," just the ability to do whatever felt good.

### MORNING MEDITATION AND A NEW SPIRIT GUIDE

While lying in bed with the windows open to allow a soft breeze to enter the room, I felt all my chakras open; I could sense a shift in the energy around me in a very clear, distinct way. Suddenly, before me appeared the face of young Native American woman with long dark hair and beautiful, large dark eyes. The whole room lit up brightly, surrounding her with light. She told me she was associated with this sacred area and was here to guide me, adding that my power and acceleration would increase quite a bit being in Sedona. She said:

***"Every experience you have changes you significantly and there's no going back."***

She then showed me the image of an electronic item being taken apart so as to see what comprises it:

*"The deeper you go in, seeing each individual component, the deeper your understanding becomes."*

She showed me an image of picking up one grain of sand and seeing how, even in this case, one can still go deeper and see that it's made up of smaller particles. I then watched as the grain transformed into a web that interconnects the Universe and everything in it.

What a powerful way to start my day!

## THE BIRTHING CAVE

I decided to spend Easter visiting a sacred healing vortex site called the Birthing Cave. I'd never been there before, and it now seemed especially appropriate, given that this was a time of rebirth for me.

As I drove up the road toward the trailhead, a large raven flew right over my car as if to lead the way. The vortex was a little tricky to find because after a certain point there was neither road signage nor clear markers on the trail, just many different paths. I just had to trust that I was headed in the right direction, which of course I was.

After my hike, I stopped by a nearby shop and bought myself an angel aura necklace in the shape of an upside-down triangle that represented the Divine feminine and symbolized the womb. Rebirth seemed to be the theme of the day, for sure.

Then, while at Whole Foods to pick up my dinner, I heard ELO's "Strange Magic" playing on the loudspeaker. So appropriate! As I put my basket on the belt to check out, the woman behind the register waved her hand at me and I thought I heard her say something to me quietly, but indiscernibly. When I asked her to repeat her message, she replied, "I didn't say anything, but I was about to!" Apparently, I was reading her energy and hearing her psychically before the words actually came out of her mouth. She saw I was wearing my Evoke Meditation shirt and laughed, saying, "I guess you could read my energy because you're well meditated!"

On the road back to the cabin, I was reminded of a recent reading I'd given, during which the woman's grandfather and father came through to offer messages. The word "cradle" came up, along with this message from Spirit: ***"Allow us to lift the weight from your shoulders and to cradle and care for you now."*** At the time, I'd thought that was so sweet for her loved ones to say to her, but today it was a message being given to me as well.

Indeed, I had spent the day in nature's cradle – the birthing cave – which, again, was specifically where I wanted to be on Easter Sunday. I just savored my time there, and so did about fifteen other people (and a few dogs), with everyone laughing, smiling, and basking together as a community of strangers who came together to celebrate this day and honor this sacred space. When someone was struggling to climb up or down within the cave, everyone lent a hand. It was just beautiful!

Back at the ranch, I sat outside by the walking labyrinth, under a tree with Tibetan flags and chimes waving in the gentle breeze. Enjoying the warmth from the late-afternoon sun, I closed my eyes for a meditation and saw my new spirit guide, as well as my psychic guide, who kept repeating the word "SACRED."

She said, ***"This is a sacred time, a sacred place, for sacred ritual in a sacred land."***

Afterward, while writing down some notes, I realized my phone's camera had somehow opened on its own, capturing an image of the chair's handle! It looked just like a nautilus – a symbol in sacred geometry of the Fibonacci golden spiral representing spiritual evolution. I then received the following download:

> ***Each "chamber" or place you go offers you a learning experience and when you outgrow one of the chambers or places, you move on to the next one.***

In that moment, I could feel goosebumps, which I call "truth chills," running all over my arms. It felt like the smaller pieces of this puzzle I'd been trying to figure out were finally starting to come together to create the bigger picture of this journey I was on.

I loved the energy of Sedona. Here, I felt so clear-minded and more firmly rooted in who I am, what I want (and don't want), and what I'll allow for myself moving forward. I felt solid in my own inner power and inner knowing.

# DAY THIRTY-ONE

After my morning meditation, I had breakfast and coffee while rewatching a movie I love – Caroline Cory's *Superhuman.* I had left off on the part where they talk about the power of thought and sound. They showed the visual effect and manifestation of the words we speak. It was a great reminder that:

***Words are powerful, so choose and use them intentionally.***

***Your words are a reflection of your thoughts and these also create your reality.***

***Even if you don't speak aloud you are still communicating to the Universe and they are "heard."***

Just then, I had the "thought" of having truth chills just before actually feeling them. I smiled and thanked my spirit team for always being with me and for me, and then I began to feel really emotional and overwhelmed. However, this time it wasn't a feeling of sadness, but rather an immense appreciation for where I'm at now and how far I've come to get here in my life. Looking around this tiny cabin on this desert ranch in the middle of nowhere, I felt more at home than ever before. That feeling didn't come from being in a particular place, but rather it was coming home to myself and feeling truly connected to Source and Spirit.

I felt more understanding and accepting of myself, in all my uniqueness, than I ever have. In the past, I'd always say, "I'm just weird that way," which is what I felt from everyone around me. Now, I knew that what seemed weird to everyone else was normal for me, and I was ready to embrace, embody, and consciously tap into it. It was my entire purpose for being here in this life.

As always, the Psychic Tarot Oracle cards perfectly reflected what was happening in my life.

**Spiritual Strength**

In this image, Spirit is literally raising and holding up
the ceiling on behalf of a monk to take the weight and
burden off his shoulders and clear the path.
This represents "courage, discipline, stability, and
persistence... you've been through so much to get
to this point; and even though you may have acquired
some scars from the battle, you're wiser and
stronger for it." It reminded me of the words
in the reading the other day:
***"Allow us to lift the weight from your shoulders and***
***to cradle and care for you now."***

**Fertility/ The Empress**

Giving birth to a new creation
Cradled and held in the womb
Not yet ready for birth, but being fertilized
be patient as you watch your seeds
take root and grow.
Open yourself to the life force of the Universe.
As you interact with others now, even if you're in
the midst of solving a problem, use gentle care and
kindness as you handle such situations.
Act from a loving space of your heart center.

# DAY THIRTY-THREE

Last night I had a "moment"... well, more like a mini- meltdown. Just before bed, worry and frustration started coming up over the fact that I was over a month into this journey and, though I'd gained some clarity, so much was still unknown. I wanted more support, connection, and direction on where to go next and what to do. Then, after getting ready for bed, I put on some angelic healing tunes and laid down to comfort and soothe myself as I allowed some tears to flow.

I woke in very early morning and called in the guides and angels to draw near. I telepathically communicated that I truly appreciated all their support, but I did want and need more balance of my spiritual practice with companionship, comfort, and support in the physical world.

I received the following response:

***"This is a SACRED TIME***
***You are being held in the womb in this sacred space.***
***It feels like there's no movement from your point of view,***
***but there's actually a lot happening behind the scenes***
***to prepare you and to create the dream that you desire.***

***This is a time for shedding old beliefs and patterns.***
***Things need to come up and out in this time***
***of cleansing and renewal."***

Surrounded by a feeling of unconditional love and support, I was able to fall right back into a restful sleep.

Later that morning, I received a text from the ranch owner – who I had bonded with during my earlier stay – offering me access to a larger empty cabin for the next couple of days to use as an office space! She also invited me on a morning hike. I felt like my prayer from last night was being answered already!

After finishing my mediumship group, I changed and headed out to run some errands. Then, instead of going straight into Sedona proper for a hike as I'd been doing each day, I felt called to go to Cottonwood. On the drive out, I saw a man with a large camping backpack walking on the road alone. I started to pass him, but then felt the need to stop and make sure he was okay, see if he needed a ride. He was so happy and thankful and said most people didn't bother to stop. He told me his name was Chris, and as we chatted for a bit I was surprised and delighted to learn he had started his journey in Charlotte, North Carolina – what a small world! He had completed his time in the Army and was now on a soul journey too. He started by driving cross-country, but ended up parking his car in Phoenix and walking through Hopi land all the way to Sedona! Amazing!

Of course, Chris was headed to Cottonwood, which explained why I'd felt the need to go there first today. He hopped in, and we had a blast talking and listening to some tunes as we rolled down the road, marveling at how our crazy adventures had merged together. It struck me again how Spirit was directly and swiftly answering my prayer for more support, connection, and direction in the physical. Perhaps Chris had uttered the same request, for he was so eager to speak about life with someone who spoke the same language.

I took him all the way to his destination and gave him some cash to help with his travel expenses. Then we hugged, agreeing that we'd most likely see each other again somewhere down the road. It felt so magical to have drawn him into my experience, but that's how it works – people like us are brought together at exactly the right time.

# DAY THIRTY-FIVE

This morning while having breakfast, I watched an interview with Raymond Moody. He was talking about how most people understandably view any difficult people or situations in their lives in a very negative way. In reality, Moody explained, this life is really just a play and we all have our parts. In the grand scheme of things, these difficult people and experiences are meant to be educational and instigators of growth. I've always felt that way. I thought back to many of the Broadway shows or operas I'd been to, recalling how the actor playing the villain often received the loudest applause at the end, once the audience was no longer caught up in the drama.

I was also reminded of the challenges I had faced in childhood, and how my mom had later apologized to me and my sister. She wished she could have done things differently to make our growing up easier. She said this more than once, and each time I would assure her that I'd chosen her as my mom before coming into this world, knowing there would be some challenges. I'd often explained that I came here to experience all aspects of life – both "good" and "bad" – in order to evolve spiritually. I would also tell her how thankful I was for all the difficult experiences I had early on.

They had definitely taken me to a dark place for a while, but within that struggle I was forced to find my connection to Source and see the world in a profoundly different way, which changed my entire life for the better. Life isn't something we can learn from reading a book, it's something we must learn firsthand. These experiences had made me a much stronger person and helped me to find my path at a much younger age than most.

I see so many young people today being coddled and shielded from everything, which denies them the opportunity to take ownership of their own mistakes and decisions and prevents them from developing independence, both in thought and action. I find this to be a huge disservice, often leading to a negative spiral of codependency within families and relationships of every kind. When you learn to let go, you allow room for greater growth and expansion. LET GO TO GROW.

Throughout my career as a Speech Language Pathologist, I have worked with clients of all ages. My job was to purposely present them with opportunities to face specific areas of difficulty with behavior or communication and learn to navigate these situations while scaffolding support so they could develop independent and functional life skills. To learn to walk and find your balance, you first have to wobble and fall.

Growth and healing also require facing uncomfortable feelings and experiences. When I was in and out of the hospital across 2017, all I could do was cry and pray to God to help me. I was already on the highest dose of meds the staff could give me and I was still lying in bed with so much pain I couldn't move. When I left the hospital, I had a huge open wound from one of my surgeries and knew this would take a lot of time to heal. I couldn't walk, I had significant swelling and inflammation throughout my body, and tubes coming out of several places as well. Despite all the medication, the pain was still significant, and you can better believe I had my meds scheduled down to the minute; otherwise, I'd be in an unbearable world of hurt beyond what I was already experiencing. However, though I still had a lot of healing and rehabilitation ahead of me, I started weaning myself off them as soon as I could to prevent any risk of dependence long-term. This meant feeling some of that pain along my healing journey while finding alternative methods to better manage it, including reviving my dedicated practice of meditation.

Like my childhood, my time in the hospital and the recovery period afterward forced me to look within for answers, as there were no solutions to be found in the outside sources around me. For that, I was grateful.

Being on this solo journey had certainly had its ups and downs so far, and it brought to light some tough memories and feelings. For that I also gave thanks for showing me what needed to be cleared. I prayed for the strength, courage, grace, and ease to move through any challenge I may face as I continued along my path.

I had the sense that I was being called to be off the grid, with little to no internet connectivity, for a reason: it was a time to go deeper within. It reminded me of my conversation with my fellow spiritual nomad, Chris. He commented that when you have your earbuds in and your music stops or your connection goes out, it means:

***"STOP AND LISTEN. PAY ATTENTION. It's not a fluke. You are meant to hear something else in that moment. Maybe it's the sounds of nature, but more likely it's something INSIDE OF YOU."***

In my travels, I had attended several workshops on various aspects of spirituality – each valuable in its own way. That said, while listening to these experts, I'd realized I was not so much a participant or student but more of an observer of their processes. None of the wisdom from their teachings was new information for me, but rather beautiful reminders of what I already knew. I realized that my purpose in being there was to trust and empower myself and bring positive uplifting energy to the group, as we all come together in a community of seekers and alternative thinkers.

At this point in my spiritual journey, the wisdom and insights I sought no longer came from outside teachers, but from my own source. Same goes for any psychic or mediumship reading – they simply served to validate the messages I was already tapping into on a daily basis. In fact, they came to me directly with much greater specificity, vibrancy, and depth when I received them for myself. As one of my mediumship mentors always asks:

***"Where are you sourcing your information?"***

In other words, always ask yourself from whom or where you're receiving guidance and feel into whether it resonates truth. Everything you seek can be found within.

Another mentor and well-known psychic medium once said to me:

> *"It seems that you and I are really just hanging out here, because I can see you already know and have received all this information, haven't you? The one piece of advice I can give is that you don't need to look to others for validation anymore."*

## DAY THIRTY-SIX

### CLOSE ENCOUNTERS WITH SPIRIT

Today I was guided to think back to the early part of my life, when I encountered spirit energies, and get a better understanding of how they've been trying for so long to get my attention. Though I had been seeking a deeper communication with Spirit for many years, I remembered like it was yesterday how terrified I was back then of any experiences with the unknown or unseen realms.

Oftentimes these experiences occurred during or around sleep, and though many were likely a reaction to the negativity I was exposed to in my physical environment, I could also clearly see a connection to my spiritual abilities. As a very young child, I was constantly waking up to nightmares. One of my earliest dream recollections was about being buried alive, which terrified me – not just because of the obvious, but because it meant I'd be there for an eternity. You see, I already had the understanding that we never really die.

I sleepwalked a lot in my youth. The next morning, the adults in the house would tell me how I got up to do rote tasks such as sitting down to play the piano or sitting on their bed until they directed me to go back to sleep.

I now believe this was my soul having left my physical body to escape the stress I was bombarded with at that time. I've talked with a couple of other psychic mediums who also said they were sleepwalkers, which has led me to wonder if this was indicative of a propensity for trance states.

I also, from a young age, frequently experienced sleep paralysis during which I would be met with dark, ominous figures looming over me. I always tried to scream or call for help, but couldn't. There were many nights I was afraid to fall asleep knowing what I would wake up to. During hypnogogic states – that groggy space between sleep and wakefulness – I would often sense beings or energy around me. For many years I was very fearful of this; I wanted to avoid interaction with spirit entities of any kind. As mentioned before, many nights, while alone in my room, I would experience panic attacks due to my alarming realization that the physical world and people around me may be just an illusion. It made me question my ability to discern what was real and what wasn't.

Very vivid dreams have been a part of my life as far back as I can remember, and as a teenager I began documenting and analyzing them every single morning. Some seemed especially real, and I later came to realize they were encounters with deceased loved ones and spirits. Also in my teens, I began lucid dreaming, where I could fly and control events and people, which was very empowering both in my sleep world and waking states.

Of course, spirits were not limited to sleep time when attempting to contact me. Once, I heard someone come through the door to our house and figured it was my mom, only to discover she was visiting with neighbors. No one was home. On another occasion, I saw a glowing ghostly white figure moving across the backyard, but at the time chalked it up to my wild imagination.

As a teenager, I would often find my fingers typing words and phrases in the air repeatedly and unconsciously. In college, after taking some sign language courses, I would notice my hands automatically signing words to myself. Other automatic kinesthetic movements came to me later, in the form of spontaneous body movements like swaying, rocking, or pendulum-like head movements during meditations.

Spirits also used electronics to communicate with me, often by turning a tv or computer on or off. Once I heard my iPhone ringing and picked it up, shocked to see that I was receiving a call from ME, my own number! How does that even happen?

I have a close relationship with the Elementals and nature, so it's very typical to see animals behaving in strange or unexpected ways such as the cardinal or other birds watching me or swooping in front of my car to get my attention. Interestingly, I once noticed an imprint of a face and torso on a window screen of the house in Raleigh, which looked like a spirit had been peering inside! This happened to appear in the same timeframe and location that the little red cardinal first tried to find me.

I've often thought that people around me could sense this connection with Spirit, and I'm very cognizant of how others reflect my energy and how I'm feeling. This is especially evident with kids, who are much more sensitive or receptive to it. I love it when I see a baby or younger child staring at me with wide eyes as if they can see my aura or inner light, or perhaps a spirit or angel around me.

My friend's young son was particularly drawn to me, and whenever I visited he would monopolize the time until she said, "Hey, it's my turn to hang out with Aunt Jen!" He even told me once that he planned to marry me, which I thought was funny, cute, and a bit strange, considering he was about five years old!

These encounters with children have continued to this day. At a grocery store in Mount Shasta, a little boy around seven years old spontaneously greeted me with a loud "Hi!" then started chatting away as if he'd known me forever. A few minutes later, his mom came over with her jaw dropped in disbelief. "He never talks to anyone, even at home!" she exclaimed, "Really!" She could not stop smiling and eventually had to pull him away because he just kept on talking with me. He left smiling and waving, saying "Have a great day!" I definitely did, after that sweet encounter!

While at an airport in Denver waiting in line to order coffee, a mom in front of me was holding her baby, who looked to be under a year old. He turned to me, smiled, waved, and said, "Hi!" His mom gasped and said, "Oh my gosh, I can't believe he just said hi to you. He's only said that once before since he's not really talking yet."

Even at this ranch outside Sedona, I had made a new friend – the grandson of the owner, who lived with his mom in another guesthouse. After being introduced to me, he decided to come over on his own to visit as I sat outside on my patio. In fact, he didn't wanna leave and attempted to negotiate more time as his mother repeatedly tried calling him back home.

What energies within and around me are these kids picking up on? What messages are these receiving? I realize now that throughout my life I was receiving a lot through my clairsentience, in the form of feelings and kinesthetic movement, as well as clairaudience and claircognizance. Initially, I didn't realize that this was inspired by or coming from a different source, because both clairaudience and claircognizance can seem like your own thoughts. I just figured I had a strange way of working things out through conversations with myself, or that when I just knew or sensed something other people couldn't, they simply lacked some good ol' common sense. Whatever I knew or sensed felt so natural and obvious to me, but apparently it wasn't as "common" as I thought – it was claircognizance!

It's pretty typical for children to be highly intuitive and able to sense things beyond the physical realm. However, they are usually taught to believe that this is just their imagination and eventually they buy into it. This is why most adults today are completely oblivious to their own innate intuitive capabilities. Most people are encaged by the dense physical "reality" of our world, limited by what they can see and feel with their 3D senses and believing that this is all there is.

The irony is that this physical "reality" is actually the illusion and there are worlds beyond this veil for us to experience! Welcome to my world.

A huge turning point with these close encounters with Spirit, and one of my most cherished memories, was the time I was visited by my Korean grandfather. Though I'd never met him in the physical – he passed away in Korea when my mom was only sixteen – I had always felt a very close connection to him. I even had his framed picture on my coffee table, one of the few photos my mom had of him.

The visit occurred many years ago, during one of the lowest points in my adult life. I was living alone in my Raleigh townhome, feeling scared and wishing for support. One evening, I was lying on the couch, having cried myself to sleep. This was just after my divorce. I had been married for 6 years and had known right from the start it wasn't meant to be long term. I was now 32 years old and I knew I wanted something very different for my life than what I was experiencing, but the problem was I didn't know what that was yet.

My family had made it known that they didn't agree with my decision to get a divorce. They didn't understand why I was so unhappy or how I could break the sanctity of the marriage I'd committed myself to. Funny because I think the more shocking event should have been the fact that I got married at all, let alone at the tender age of 25! This was never in the cards for me, at least not ones I'd ever seen. I was never the girl that grew up imagining being married, settling down and having kids. I mean I wanted to be in a loving relationship and maybe adopt kids one day, but my dream was to travel the world and to be independent and free. And then if I somehow made it to my 40's, I'd consider marriage. This was a stark contrast to the traditional values and expectations of my family. So I can see why it was so difficult for them to wrap their heads around how someone could want something so different, and then worse, would throw it away once they had gotten on board that train. You would have thought they'd have known by then that when it comes to me, the one thing you can expect is that I'll do the unexpected both in the marriage and then later in the divorce. But, no, they even kept the pictures up from our wedding until I politely, but firmly asked that they respectfully take these down.

The irony was that initially, my family didn't understand why I married him in the first place. He was sweet, but everyone and their dog could clearly see we were an odd match. Even my ex-husband said this once before we were married when we almost broke up. However, once everyone had gotten to know him, they grew attached to him and now admonished my decision to leave! It just goes to show how you can never please people so you may as well stop trying. It's so important for every individual to learn to tune out the opinions of everyone around them, tap into the voice of their own heart and discern for themselves whether or not to work to shift the dynamic of a relationship or release it altogether.

I already felt guilty for any hurt I'd caused my ex husband despite the fact that I knew without a shadow of a doubt that it was the right choice. And, in that moment, lying there on the couch of my Raleigh townhome, I was feeling alone.

Suddenly, I woke with a start to find a dark- haired man standing on the other side of my living room. My heart started racing – how had he gotten in?! Before I could move, he started walking toward me and I felt the fear ramp up, only to realize that he was bringing a blanket to cover me. In that instant, the fear melted into a knowing that I was unconditionally loved and supported and I was being comforted by this beautiful spirit... I knew this was my H*arabaji!* My grandpa!

I fell back to asleep, wrapped in my warm blanket of love, and woke the next morning with a major epiphany. Some of the spirits I'd been fearing and keeping at bay this whole time might actually be loving entities!

This opened up a whole new way of viewing the energies I'd been sensing for so long.

## INSPIRED WRITING

When life seems quiet, like not much is going on, that's often when the most profound growth is actually occurring. The same happens when you are too close to something – it can be harder to see the whole picture. A good example of this is the parents of some of my younger speech therapy clients. They often wouldn't see the progress to the extent that I could see it, until I showed them the data comparing where their child had started to where they were presently. When they stepped back and looked at their child through a different lens, they were able to see all the growth that had taken place.

This is what my time in Sedona felt like – it was lovely and peaceful, but with not a whole lot of external forward movement. The download I received was that this was a time of preparation, similar to the process of marinating your food. If you stood there and watched it, getting aggravated that it wasn't marinating faster, the process would be very frustrating; you might even prematurely end the process and the meal wouldn't come out as good. Rather than feeling impatient about the speed with which I was moving on this journey, I needed to allow myself sufficient time to "marinate" in this new energy. Yes, it would take more time and patience, but it will result in a more savory and enjoyable result. (Hmm, as I wrote this it must have almost been mealtime, because I was beginning to feel hungry!)

In my afternoon meditation, when I asked my guides what they wanted to communicate with me today, they expanded on this same humorous analogy:

*Yes! Allow yourself to be marinated!*
*Immerse yourself in it... bathe in it... sit in it.*
*You're in gestation in this tiny Sedona artist's cabin.*
*Think of it like your cocoon as you are preparing to take flight.*

## DAY THIRTY-SEVEN

The **FERTILITY** card came up yet again in my morning tarot reading. It reminded me of the message yesterday that this artist's cabin is like a cocoon or, is this case, a womb. I was not at all surprised when, as I wrote this, a song called "Grow" began to play on my computer.

This afternoon, I had a beautiful Intuitive Healing session with Kymberley Griffin, owner of Sedona Healing Energy. I was so impressed with her healing space and, more importantly, her presence and her process. I could actually feel shocks of electricity when she touched her hands to my head, helping me release old energy. The whole session just felt so good. She talked with me about my past, including various traumas, and noted some energetic buildup. I had, as people say, "done the work" to address a lot of that stuff, so nothing felt majorly transformative today. Yet, she was definitely hitting all the right targets and tapping into places where specific events would have stored or blocked energy: my pelvis area or sacral area (sexuality, creative expression), solar plexus (emotional center and personal power), and down to my root sacra (safety, groundedness), which I knew related to feeling a lack of safety in my past and sexual trauma from the rape in my late teens.

There was also some discussion about my childhood and how we can carry "inherited" energy into this life. I was already fully aware of this and believed it came into play, specifically with my mom's ancestry and experience. It was heavy stuff, for sure, but Kymberley was able to create such a safe space for opening up that I felt joyful throughout the entire process.

She then pulled out a deck she had created and had me choose a card. It depicted a healed masculine energy and had to do with transformation and balancing the feminine and masculine within, which also spoke directly to my feeling of transformation and rebirth here.

During the session, Kymberley commented that she sensed a very angelic energy coming from me and that my role in this life is to be a teacher.

When I was on the way out the door, a huge yellow butterfly flew right around me, hovered there for a minute, and then flew off. Kymberley told me it was a yellow swallowtail and I should look up the spiritual meaning of this totem animal because it had a message for me. Later, my search results included the following words:

Rebirth
Spiritual Transformation
Communication from Ancestors
Protection
Guidance
Support
Hope

## DAY THIRTY-EIGHT

I took a shower and put on warm clothes, then sat in the chair under my favorite tree and listened to the beautiful sounds of nature. After about a minute of mindful breathing, I felt my whole body vibrating as if the ground under me was shaking or someone was physically moving my chair. I also sensed a powerful being standing right behind me; I could even feel its heart beating blending with mine. It was incredible!

I recognized the presence as one of my spirit guides – a large Native American man who had also appeared in my reading with Michael. He said I feel the energy in Sedona so strongly because I'm from here, or at least I was in a past life. I have roots here. He showed me the image of growing roots from my feet down through the Earth. I received the insight from my spirit guide that some roots are good, but others (like cords) can hold you down or keep you stuck and need to be cut. He talked to me about the stages we go through in our development and soul growth:

**STAGE 1**- *You move from victimhood to empowerment – set boundaries, stand up for yourself, speak your truth and express yourself to others.*

**STAGE 2** – *You get to a place where you are able to forgive others who have harmed you and can release old hurts so they no longer have a hold on you.*

**STAGE 3** – *You see the lessons in each experience and can appreciate them, even the challenging ones.*

**STAGE 4- MASTERY**

*You no longer see the need to forgive because you see that all of this was pre-planned and understand that we're all playing a part in this beautiful creation: the play of life. You realize that the differences we all have are a necessary part of creation. We're all connected and come from the same Source, but we all have different ideas, preferences, and interests, et cetera, and that's what expands us and the Universe.*

Then he told me that I'm here to serve as a bridge between the two worlds, the spiritual and physical:

**You see what others can't see**
**You hear what others won't hear**
**You understand what others don't yet comprehend**
**You will help others through your gifts.**
**You will help them reconnect with their own inner wisdom.**

He clearly explained that the central purpose for this soul trip was to give me the space and time to strengthen my relationship with Spirit and learn to fully trust my own inner knowing and intuition.

This journey was forcing me to "wait" and tune in to receive guidance on where to go next, trusting that I'd be led to the right place at the right time. I was already receiving more clearly than ever before. I could feel all of my senses opening up, the door blown wide open!

CHAPTER SIX

# OBSTACLES AND CHALLENGES

***"Obstacles, power struggles, and challenges that you must face in order to overcome them. Don't get caught up in it, just pause and stand back for clarity."***

**~ by John Holland**
**The Psychic Tarot Oracle Deck**

# DAY THIRTY-NINE

I woke several times in middle of the night and jotted down the following vivid dreams:

DREAM #1

I'm walking down a long dirt road. There's a woman here and several students. The trail is lined with art and I comment on how beautiful it is. Someone asks the woman to give readings for everyone. She walks down the road, but then turns to me and says to: "Follow the voice within."

DREAM #2

I'm walking on a path and come across a class in which the teacher is reviewing the key takeaways so far. I'm looking at one of the rock formations and see myself sitting inside a hole that looks just like the birthing cave womb. I'm sitting with my legs crossed meditating and smiling.

These were such clear messages and imagery about my path and showing me what my future would entail including the offering of psychic mediumship readings, teaching, and somehow incorporating my artwork- all for the purpose of offering inspiration and healing for others. However, the second dream was a reminder that right now everything was still in the gestation process and I needed to allow more time before this would all come to fruition. For now, I needed to continue to follow and trust my inner knowing....that still small voice, which was guiding me to the next right step on my path, further down the road towards my destiny.

## STARSEEDS

On my way to my usual trail, I felt the still small voice within nudging me to make a pitstop to a used bookstore. This message came in the blink of an eye, just as I was about to pass the turn-off, and my hands – seemingly without my express say-so – turned my car's steering wheel left in the direction it wanted me to go.

You know it's guidance when it's a "no-brainer." It's no longer your own thought or coming from your own mind alone. You just automatically want or are guided to do something without planning or logic.

Once there, I took a straight path for their metaphysical section in the back of the store. After taking my time to look through the rows of books and stacking up a few to purchase, a young girl (probably in her twenties) who I had noticed eyeing me, walked over. She shared that she suddenly felt called to recommend a specific book to me, then reached over and pulled it off the shelf. I looked down at the cover and saw the title: *STARSEED, The Third Millennium: Living in the Posthistoric World,* by Ken Carey. Somehow, it seemed familiar to me though I'd never read it or seen it before.

The young woman told me the book contained channeled information, adding that some topics were really odd for most people. I smiled to myself, thinking she obviously wasn't entirely clear on who she was talking to - odd is my normal! I had, literally, been reading channeled books before she was born, since my teen years, when I immersed myself in all things metaphysical. Books often seemed to be jumping off the shelf at me, including the whole collection of *Seth Books,* channeled by Jane Roberts. This series had resonated as truth and felt like a breath of fresh air. What a relief it was to finally find something that actually made sense to me when nothing else in my life did.

She then said that some people might come out of it thinking they are separate or at a higher level than others, so I should be aware of that. I felt that both caveats were unnecessary, but I was so grateful that she'd been guided to lead me to this information. I sincerely thanked her for being a conduit and added it to my stack of books, already excited and intrigued at what I might find inside!

# DAY FORTY

After my workday, I immediately drove to Boynton Canyon Trail, thinking I'd try out the new path that led to a cave I'd been reading about. There was an "old path" and a "new path," and I decided I'd wait until I reached the fork and see which way I was drawn.

Little did I know I was in for a day of lessons – almost like a mini spiritual bootcamp.

Sure enough, when I got to the fork I felt something pull me toward the "new" path – and the cave – so that's the way I went. There was a good bit of trust involved, since the path was unmarked and appeared to have a few possible trails, not all of which led to the same place. But once I arrived I was so glad *I* had been led there. The cave area was amazing to behold!

**OBSTACLE # 1**

There was a huge upward climb; it was pretty high and steep, like a slide, with no real footholds. As I made my way up, I could feel myself having to find balance and ways to grip. Other people were climbing to the top quickly and with apparent ease, and I knew I could climb up as well. Yet, I found myself stopping at the midway point. My concern: how would I get down if I had to do it the same way??!!

After pausing for a good long moment, hemming and hawing, I ended up climbing back down and heading back on the path. I just didn't quite feel up to it today. Come to think of it, even when I started on my usual trail, I wasn't quite feeling myself – not very energetic, a little jittery, hungry, tired, and bit weak. I didn't even feel like I wanted to hike the entire trail, though I'd practically ran it every previous day this week.

Still, as I walked back along the path, I pondered why I would suddenly feel a sense of fear or worry when normally I would have forged ahead without a second thought. My feeling of being "off" when I started the trail had only intensified because I hadn't made it to the top to see the view. Should I have turned around? Why was I hesitant?"

I then recalled a couple of conversations I'd overheard the day before while at one of the local shops. One gentleman said something about "marinating an idea," which made my ears perk up because it was the exact analogy and wording my spirit guides had just given to me. Then they were talking about the lunar eclipse that was happening and how some people would really feel its powerful effects. He said it was time of transformation to "shed the old skin," clear old beliefs, and patterns to clear the way for the new. Okay, perhaps this eclipse had something to do with how I was feeling.

On the one hand, I felt good that regardless of what other people were doing I had chosen what was best for me today; on the other hand, I didn't like not making it to the top. I also began to feel as though this was a set-up for a lesson of some kind... that I was guided to this situation for some kind of learning about myself.

**OBSTACLE # 2**

On my way back to my car, a man in front of me suddenly stopped in the middle of the path. At my questioning look, he pointed ahead and told me there were a whole bunch of javelinas – often confused with wild boars and commonly found in Arizona – slowly crossing the path. How interesting to have another obstacle come up! The only thing we could do was patiently wait it out. Well, technically, we did have other choices but since javelinas can be quite aggressive, especially when they have babies with them, it was definitely best to take a pause until the route was clear and safe again.

**OBSTACLE # 3**

At the grocery store I got a cart that was not rolling as easily as it should. It was not stuck, but it was a lot harder to push forward. And of course you don't realize it until you're already halfway in the store, so I just kept rolling with it, half-laughing about yet another obstruction. This was starting to become a pattern…

**OBSTACLE # 4**

While driving down the dirt road to the ranch, I saw a trailer that had gotten stuck and was blocking the road, as were some other cars.

What was going on today?? The great thing is that I didn't get frustrated or mad. It was more like viewing it from the outside and truly being curious, wanting to clearly understand why I was encountering these blocks. "Okay, spirit team," I asked, "What am I supposed to learn from this? What is the lesson here for me. I would love some guidance."

As soon as the trailer was hauled to the side of the road and I continued the long drive back to the ranch, I again began to feel a sense of uncertainty about my purpose on this journey creeping up on me. Here I was, alone, with no friends, family, partner or pet to support me. And what did I really have to offer the world, anyway? When the tears came I didn't fight them; I knew better than to try bottling any emotions. I needed to let all the uncertainty, sadness, loneliness – whatever I was feeling in the moment – come up and out. Then, once I'd calmed and turned the corner with my car, what do you suppose Spirit threw out at me…?

**OBSTACLE # 5**

Seriously?! Yep, one more thing blocking my path – only this time it was an adorable baby calf! It turned to look right at me, then walked over to my car, slowly sniffed, and licked the hood before sauntering back to the front. There it turned and stopped right in the middle of the road, as if taunting me. All I could do was laugh and soak in the humor, the absurdity and, of course, the cuteness. This turned out to be a welcomed roadblock.

When I finally got back to the cabin, I closed my eyes to tune in and see what clarity might come through on my day's events. Then, I opened my laptop and did some automatic writing, which entailed the following:

*Sometimes you're going to have a block in the road or something obstructing you, slowing you down. It's not the end of the world and you don't have to get upset about it. You have to learn to just be patient, knowing it's temporary and when the timing is right and things are good to go, you'll be on the move again. Sometimes the pause can be a blessing. That little baby calf was a sweet loving messenger and an example of how sometimes a block in the road can be a good thing. Sometimes you need to slow down.*

*Being here in Sedona for two weeks, you've felt like you're not doing as much as you should and like you want to be making more movement. However, you are being guided to stay here "in the womb" for a little longer as you're still marinating, gestating, cooking in the oven. You need more time, but growth is happening, for sure.*

*We're not meant to go down every path or get to the end destination before we're ready. There is no end, anyway. Just because it's the right path for somebody else doesn't mean it's right for you. You have to feel it out and do what feels good to you in the moment.*

**LEARN TO EMBRACE THE UNKNOWN<br>THE UNCOMFORTABLE<br>EMBRACE THE MISTAKES, THE MISSTEPS, THE FAILURES<br>because they're your greatest teachers and are<br>for your highest good, even if you can't see it at the time.**

# DAY FORTY-ONE

I was inspired to arrive just a little bit early to my shamanic healing session with Kymberley, looking forward to another wonderful experience.

When I walked in, she said she had just been thinking how it would be great if I could come a little earlier to go over our intentions before my session – and here I was!

"Well, of course you'd come early!" she said, laughing. "You're a psychic medium…you heard my thoughts!"

Today, the card chosen from her tarot deck was **BALANCE**, which happened to be the same theme of the card I'd chosen that morning from my Psychic Tarot deck.

Kymberley's ears perked up when I told her about the obstacles I'd experienced the day before. She asked for more specifics, then shared that calves or cows symbolize transformation and were signs to ***tread lightly*** *on your path as you carefully consider your next step. It's a reminder to balance what you're giving and what you're receiving.* Funny, because that exact same phrase ("tread lightly") had come out of my mouth yesterday while talking about the cows to the manager of the ranch!

The javelina on my hiking trail also had spiritual significance, Kymberley explained. They were not warnings, but in fact were considered signs of special protection and reassurance. In other words, ***what sometimes appears to be an unwanted obstacle may turn out to be very positive as it's protecting you on your path.***

Furthermore, the inner voice warning me not to go further up the canyon wasn't a block to bypass and push through. It was my awareness trying to guide me to safety and protect me from a potentially tricky or harmful situation, especially on a day I wasn't feeling my strongest.

For today's healing session, I set the intention to release any old ancestral lineage energies, any old energy or emotions related to sexual trauma, completely release any baggage fully and completely, and to fully embrace my beautiful sensuality, sexuality, and physical connection for any future romantic partner. I wanted to release anything holding me back in any possible way and completely open my heart to love.

As Kymberley moved to my throat chakra the lights suddenly went out! She exclaimed aloud, "Whoa, that's weird!" Later we both laughed, saying we should know better by now than to call anything on our lives "weird!"

At another point during the healing, I heard her gasp. I didn't realize it at the time, but she went to grab her camera and snap a picture. Later, she explained that I was glowing with an intense light she'd never witnessed before in any of her healings.

During the healing, I felt a burst of energy come up and out of my throat and felt my mouth open for me as if being moved by some other gentle force. I thought someone might actually start speaking through me! I also felt my hands heat up intensely and energy vibrating throughout my body as she was working on me. We were really in sync, because just before she gave an instruction of what to visualize, I was already doing it.

It felt as though only ten minutes had passed when she told me our hour-long session was finished. Kymberley gave me a beautiful heart-to-heart hug, and I left feeling like we would stay connected. She does such beautiful unique healing work and I have much respect for her. She said that if I lived here she'd have to hire me to work with her... so tempting!

## DAY FORTY-TWO

Early in the afternoon, I headed for a local laundromat in Cottonwood. As I waited for the dryer to finish, I was inspired to treat myself to a reading. Though I was receiving and trusting my inner guidance more than ever, I thought it would be fun to connect with another psychic and experience their unique way of reading.

I searched some places online and narrowed it down to two readers in Sedona. One didn't do in-person readings and wasn't available until the following day. The other intuitive, Annie Abbott, worked out of a local store and also didn't appear to have any openings that day; yet as I read her profile I felt very drawn to her. When I called the store to see if there was someone else who could read me, I was surprised and delighted to learn Annie *was* there and available right when I wanted to come! A little while later, I was seated across from her and having a fantastic reading. Turned out, she had trained at the same places I have, and even with some of the same teachers! Clearly, I'd chosen a good match...or rather, was guided to her.

Annie could sense right away that I was already doing this work too. In fact, I had been receiving numerous requests for psychic or mediumship readings, especially since coming to Sedona. Kymberley had referred multiple people to me, including her sister. I truly appreciated that people were trusting me in that way, and loved that Annie was picking up on it. After pulling my tarot cards, she jumped right in to explain what she was seeing for me.

"This is a time of a lot of unknowns for you," she said, "but you need to trust that you already have the tools you need. Right now you're in a nesting period. Allow yourself to be nurtured and be loving with yourself, especially as emotions are flowing as part of your healing." So far, her message, and even her wording, was spot on to my experience!

"You are definitely surrounded by and work with the Archangels!" Annie said. "I can also see here that you're a healer and have been in past lives, so you brought this natural ability forward with you into this life. You are able to offer angelic healing and you may be teaching this at a future time. Writing will also be a part of the work you do to share your teachings. You have many tools in your toolbox and can use all of these, more like a spiritual coach versus only having one specialty."

With regard to obstacles, Annie talked about how it was important to follow my guidance as it was there to keep me safe on my path.

***"It's important that we listen when we get a warning or feel like pausing or even turning around. This isn't giving in to fear, it's being wise and intuitively guided."***

I felt a really great connection with Annie and she gave me her email address to stay in touch, especially if I had any questions. Who knows... we may even see each other in one of our mediumship circles! Either way, I was so grateful to, once again, be divinely guided to exactly the right person who could deliver clear and accurate messages and support.

That evening, back at the ranch, I said my goodbyes to the owner, who was leaving for a trip early the next morning. I think of her as not just a friend, but a soul sister with the same overarching purpose of offering healing, leadership, and spiritual teaching. She hugged me, saying how brave I was for taking a journey most wouldn't even consider.

"I just don't think I'd be able to do it," she said, "even if I had the choice and didn't have this ranch to tend to."

Her words, like Annie's, were extra confirmation of what I already knew. This journey was a lengthy and often challenging exercise in being one-hundred percent in surrender mode, being fully committed to my path, and trusting my inner guidance, that's for sure!

## DAY FORTY-THREE

While preparing breakfast, I pulled up a video on starseeds to learn more about this fascinating concept and Ken Carey's book. To that point, I'd only gotten as far as his introduction.

As a child, I always felt very drawn to astronomy and the stars. The film *2001: A Space Odyssey* was instantly a favorite of mine as it felt more like a disclosure of some truths that were being revealed to me about the Universe rather than some manufactured science "fiction." Most people loved Stanley Kubrick's 1968 cult classic because it stepped outside the usual film structure; I was hooked on the way it so beautifully connected science with spirituality and consciousness. It was one of the things that prompted my love of physics, which I majored in when I first went off to college.

As I listened to a discussion about Andromedans, I remembered my dad telling me that he'd almost named me either Andromeda or Cassiopeia! I don't know how you get from Andromeda to Jennifer, but I also don't believe in coincidences. His original inspiration for his daughter's name had to be significant in some way.

As a woman in the video explained about starseeds and their purpose for incarnating here, I suddenly started to tear up, which surprised even me. With a start, I recalled waking from a dream that morning, in which I was given the following message:

***"An aforementioned event will result in an emotional release."***

At the time I received this dream message, I didn't know what that meant and didn't recall what the "aforementioned event" was. Now, though, it seemed these truths I was hearing, combined with these recollections of earlier events in my life, were triggering an emotional response. It felt like seeds that had been planted long ago were now opening and beginning to activate some deeper knowing within me. It wasn't lost on me that just the other day I had asked to gain clarity on who I am, where I come from, and what my purpose is.

As I watched more videos and listened to people identifying themselves as one or more various categories of starseeds, I found myself getting really turned off by the separation mentality. Every video seemed to have a theme of labeling, comparing, and marginalizing different groups – just as the girl at the bookstore had mentioned. Though I still felt the warning was unnecessary for me, I now clearly understood why she felt the need to say it.

My intention was to better understand my purpose, continue to expand my knowledge of anything that would help me on my path, and to tap into and utilize this connection with higher intelligence so I could translate it into this life experience and do my part to share it with others. As I was contemplating this, my clairaudience began buzzing with tones and my head was tingling. I paused to listen to what my inner voice was trying to communicate with me:

*There are some that will separate themselves with this knowledge. However, you can use this knowledge to your advantage and gain a stronger sense of connection and purpose.*

*You are opening up further and expanding your awareness to other resources of intelligence, including us! We have been here waiting for you to be ready and now is the time.*

*You are in the prime place for this and we will continue to communicate with you further on your journey if you're open to it. . . .*

*We encourage you to BE OPEN.*
*CONTINUE TO OPEN UP AND EXPAND*

*Don't get caught up on the details for now.*

*Just know that it's a much more diverse world than people currently understand or believe.*

*EXPAND YOUR CONSCIOUSNESS*
*If you are open, we will work with you.*
*We already have been.*

Then I was shown an image of me falling into a soft net – symbolic of their arms, their support – which made me well up with emotion.

***ALLOW YOURSELF TO RECEIVE***
***TRUST***
***FALL INTO OUR ARMS***
***WE'VE GOT YOU***
***FEEL OUR LOVE***
***YOU ARE HELD***

***You can fly free and you can trust and know that we will always catch you and cushion your fall.***

***YOU ARE SAFE***

CHAPTER SEVEN

# THE UNIVERSE

*"The same energy making up the stars in the sky,
the same energy that's coursing through the Universe,
is in each and every individual.
In ancient times, many believed that each star was the soul of one person. These "souls" shined so brightly to guide others through the darkness – and so too can your wise soul."*

**~ by John Holland**
**The Psychic Tarot Oracle Deck**

# DAY FORTY-FOUR

## Joshua Tree, CA

I had a six-hour drive through very remote off-the-beaten- path areas that took me from Sedona to Joshua Tree. They were desolate and isolated, with the exception of a few small patches of homes, trailers, some small storefronts (that didn't all look open), and, in the more "booming" areas, maybe a Dollar Tree. It reminded me of the numerous small rural North Carolina towns I had been used to seeing while living back East. Honestly, it felt a bit like I was in the Twilight Zone.

When I crossed from Arizona to California, however, the road and the light changed dramatically. It suddenly became brighter and the scenery looked soft and dreamy, as if someone pulled a filter over my eyes. The road stretched ahead of me and I could see it go on for miles and miles, with these small hills or dips on the road that added some fun to the drive. The desertscape outside my window was so unique, set against a horizon delineated by a row of harsher-looking mountains in the distance. I tried calling my friend Trish – I'd promised to on the way – but the super-spotty reception in these remote areas prevented a connection. Guess I was meant to be left alone with my thoughts and my music.

I arrived just before 4 p.m. and was pleased to see that my new temporary home actually reflected what was advertised online: peaceful, spacious, clean, modern – just what I was looking for on this next phase of my adventure. And I was really looking forward to it – Joshua Tree and the nearby town of Twentynine Palms had evolved from their military history to become a haven for artists, creatives, and people just wanting privacy and to be off the grid. Sounded like they were describing me to a

T! There was a small neighborhood grocery store a minute away from the home and a small horse ranch right across the street; plus, I had a private patio affording me a gorgeous open view of several Joshua trees marking the desert landscape behind the house. Perfect!

I went about my usual routine when arriving in a new place: grabbing groceries, unpacking, and showering; then I settled down for my evening meditation. The plan was to cook dinner afterward, but the meditation left me feeling so cozy in bed I didn't want to get up. When I finally convinced myself to return to my physical body, I felt still out of it, drowsy, like I had only partially returned. After dinner, I had absolutely no energy or desire for any work, planning, journaling, tarot, or anything except relaxing, streaming a show, pouring a glass of wine, and playing with some art. **Sometimes the most productive thing you can do for yourself is just rest!**

By 10 p.m., I was completely exhausted and ready for bed. My workday had an early start tomorrow; thank God it would also be a short, easy day. Clearly, I could use some more rest!

## DAY FORTY-FIVE

I had set my alarm for six, a little later than usual, only to wake up before five anyway. That was fine, I thought as I got up to start my day. I had awakened to some pretty intense and interesting dream messages regarding my "lineage" that I wanted to document right away.

I recalled repeatedly hearing words like "Arcturian," "galactic," and "interstellar" being spoken.

"You have experienced many incarnations," an unnamed voice told me in the dream, "as many different types of beings. You have a strong, powerful energy and light within you. You have the ability to communicate with many different beings in many different worlds."

It was a lot to take in, but I just allowed it to "marinate" and was appreciative to be getting more clarity on this whole starseed topic and how it related to me.

While having coffee and breakfast, I watched a video with Mitch Horowitz – prolific writer and speaker on spiritual topics. Aside from the fact that he's very knowledgeable and wonderfully articulate, one of the things I respect most about Horowitz is that he is a contrarian – meaning, he doesn't just blindly accept what he hears and reads but purposefully and intentionally seeks to question the norm. In pushing the boundaries of the general consensus, he helps expand the thoughts and beliefs of the collective.

I particularly love his quote, "I sacrifice conventions." Hell yes! I have always appreciated people who don't adhere to social norms and are unafraid to think and act outside the box.

Then, during an early-afternoon meditation, I received even more guidance from my guides regarding my time in Joshua Tree:

*It is still a time for rest and going deep.*
*Being in a place of isolation is still needed to rest your mind*
*and tap into your intuition even deeper. Continue to develop*
*and deepen your relationship with your Spirit Team and*
*the Angels. This is crucial, especially since you will be*
*diving into your healing work soon and they will be*
*assisting you. Take care of this physical vessel and rest*
*your overworked mind. This will bring you both peace*
*of mind and clarity when making future decisions. You have*
*an abundance of choices coming your way in all areas.*

*BE DISCERNING*
*TAKE YOUR TIME*
*ALWAYS LISTEN TO THE SMALL STILL VOICE*
*PRAY AND ASK FOR GUIDANCE.*
*You are about to take flight.*

## DAY FORTY-SIX

I woke this morning and opened the curtains to see the sun hovering on the horizon. As I went outside to welcome the day, I couldn't help but recall the feeling of unease I'd had the night before. Once again I was in an unfamiliar place, not knowing where I'd be headed next. Everything was up in the air, and those all-too-familiar thoughts, "What the hell am I doing? and "Where the hell am I going" crept in again. It was probably good I'd been in a half-drugged state, the result of exhaustion, that made it impossible to do anything but take it easy, settle in, and rest.

When I came inside, I went about getting ready for my first online work session. As I brushed my teeth, with only ten minutes to spare, I thought, "Even if I only have two minutes, I will use those two minutes to ground, connect with my higher self, and tune in before I start my workday."

Once in front of the computer, I closed my eyes to tune in.

I saw the image in my mind's eye of the HOPE card from The Psychic Tarot deck; it depicted a woman reaching and looking toward light shining down upon her. Then, while waiting for my client to log in, I pulled a card up on my app and received the THIRD EYE chakra card.

I was immediately given the download in my mind that:

***You don't actually need the tarot cards as you can "see" with your mind's eye, but these are still helpful tools, especially when working with others in your readings. This is a strong area for you as you can see beyond and it will continue to expand and grow, as will your other senses.***

***Get yourself grounded and settled here in this new land and space, even though it's temporary. This will serve you very well.***

*TRUST that you will be guided to the next step.*
*We know you feel unstable now, but you are already*
*getting clarification toward your next steps.*

*Just follow each little intuitive hit.*
*TRUST IN WHAT YOU RECEIVE*
*no matter how seemingly big or small.*
*In fact, nothing is too big or too small for us to show to you.*

This afternoon, feeling like I needed something earthly, I decided to check out a bit of the town. I soon found myself at a cute little shop about fifteen minutes away, having a fun time shopping for clothes and jewelry and chatting with the young woman behind the counter. She'd lived here for about fifteen years, she said, and I shared that I was just visiting. Yet, as I said the words, I had the sense that I could easily stay here longer. There was something about the energy of the place and the locals that resonated with me. I could possibly live here for a while, I thought, or at least return for another visit.

One of the items I purchased was a leather ring with two crisscrossed arrows in the middle surrounded with rays of light. Each arrow pointed outward in a different direction and into the great unknown, speaking to me of the crossroads I'd been faced with when starting this journey. However, when I put it on, I was inspired to turn the arrows in the only direction that matters:

*BOTH ARROWS POINTED INWARD TOWARDS ME*
*THIS IS THE DIRECTION I'M HEADED*
*NO MATTER WHERE I TRAVEL PHYSICALLY,*
*ALL ROADS LEAD ME INWARD*
*BACK TO MYSELF*

I went next door to a cool coffee shop and eatery and, again, really dug the vibe of the people there. On my way out, I caught eyes with a local who looked like an old-school punk rocker covered in tats...my people! He was holding his guitar ready to just hang out and jam. We smiled at one another and nodded with the recognition of two kindred independent spirits just quickly crossing paths.

On the way home, I stopped by another store and picked up several self-care items – lotions, facial masks, foot masks, et cetera – that I could pamper myself with in the comfort of my rental. Oh, yeah, and I got some yummy chocolate-covered almonds because… why not?!

My energy was getting better and better and I was almost staring to feel at home in Joshua Tree. I was definitely feeling much more aligned, balanced, and clear-minded. The outing had reminded me how important it is to **balance the spiritual with the physical** and take the time to ground myself more, especially with all of this movement into the unknown.

It's funny how the other day and even last night, I was so resistant and felt this block, perhaps a little fear or resistance, about opening up to these otherworldly relationships and communications. I felt very safe and protected with my familiar Archangels, guides, and spirit helpers, but wasn't yet sure how I felt about inviting in unknown beings from other planets or dimensions.

Now, I felt myself changing, expanding. I felt myself letting go of the fear and opening up to my fuller potential and I knew that meant being a communicator between worlds.

With only three full days before I was due to take to the road once again, I finally locked onto my next destination: Mount Shasta! This sacred place kept coming up in my mind whenever I considered it, so I just left it up to the Universe and trusted my gut feeling and divine timing. Then I would take action.

Funny – when I first arrived in Joshua Tree the other day and was driving through town, I'd noticed a road sign that actually read Mount Shasta and wondered if it was a "sign" for me to head there. Apparently, it literally was! I still needed to map out my route and stops along the way – it was a pretty long haul – but I wasn't worried. I knew and trusted that it would all come together.

# DAY FORTY-SEVEN

I felt tired again this morning and did not want to get up, but I had a full day of therapy sessions. As I got out of bed, I could almost hear my Army Captain dad's voice saying, "Onward and upward!"

I recalled a dream that included a visitation from a guide. The message: ***"You become activated with healing energy when you're in certain places. It's all been prewired or encoded within you."*** The dream felt so real. I felt a knowing of its truth and woke feeling happy and smiling to have received that clarity.

After opening my curtains, I saw a gorgeous orange sun just beginning to peek over the horizon. I closed my eyes, placed my hands over my heart, set my intentions, and thanked the Universe for this new day.

While having coffee and breakfast and getting ready for work, I listened to a show about near-death experiences (NDEs) as wake-up calls. It reminded me of my time in the hospital back in 2017 – an "in case of emergency" situation that I believe was pre-planned to get me on my path and back on track with my soul contract.

Just prior to this incident, I'd been stressed out, overworked, giving all my energy to others, both professionally and in my romantic relationship. I was not taking any time to care for myself. I knew there was another path for me work-wise and I was in the process of moving toward that, but I was looking to business coaches and so-called "experts," none of whom could lead me in the right direction. I had become numb to pain and was not honoring my true desires, feelings, or any of my needs.

When the Universe's subtle but persistent attempts to get my attention went ignored, It turned up the volume to full blast. That's when I ended up in the emergency room and was admitted to the intensive care unit.

During this time, I became so sensitive to pain. Prior to this, I'd prided myself on my high pain tolerance. I actually enjoyed and savored the hours invested in each of my tattoos, even the one on my ribs that I was told made most grown men weep. The process felt sacred and ceremonial and made me feel alive. I guess you could say, I'm a pretty tough broad when I need to be. I can and have taken a lot in my life; I put my head down and keep moving forward, regardless of the situation. I'm a survivor. However, this isn't always a good thing when you're staying in situations that you don't need to or are ignoring signs from your guides that would lead you to an easier path.

Suddenly, I was incredibly affected by pain – or maybe it seemed that way because the level of pain was off the charts and unlike anything I'd ever experienced before. That, coupled with my heightened receptivity and sensitivity, made for a very intense situation. It was as if the floodgates had opened, with any trauma, hurts, and stresses I'd stored and were manifesting as physical agony. I now believe my team had to take away my ability to "tolerate" or put up with the pain so I could finally FEEL IT TO RELEASE IT.

Stumped, my team of doctors turned over every rock and repeatedly ran me through every possible medical test to find an answer, but never did. I endured surgery after surgery, after which I was unable to walk or move much for some time; I also lost a good bit of my hair and so much weight that I looked anorexic. My living room couch became my makeshift hospital bed because I couldn't navigate stairs. For most of 2017 my parents took turns staying over to care for me between and during my hospitalizations. It was pretty scary, to say the least, especially for someone as fiercely independent as me.

Desperate for answers as to what was wrong or what I could do to get my life back, I had no other choice but to go within. I did so with laser focus, turning to the Source of All that Is, my Higher Self, and my spirit team, and asking them to guide me and my doctors and nurses to the right treatment.

This was a huge time of awakening for me. Literal channels were carved out within my body, and a river-like stream of unknown origin was flowing and searching for a path of least resistance out.

This was opening me up to become a channel of powerful energy, understand how healing really works, and turn me inward so I could reconnect and develop an intimate relationship with Spirit and the Divine within myself.

It forced me to turn down – even turn off – the voices of everyone around me and tune into the voice within that would no longer be ignored. It required me to trust my own intuition and take better care of myself, my soul, and this beautiful vessel that houses my spirit – and understand the relationship between the two.

It opened me up to appreciating the little things and little successes – being able to walk and drive again, and being able to wear clothes without wires hanging out of me – an attitude that further assisted my healing.

During this time, I began meditating religiously – at least two times a day, every day. I felt such a strong movement of energy all throughout and around my body. My vibration was raising and my body was literally being moved kinesthetically in the process. It was if I was a car up on the blocks in the mechanic's shop, getting a complete overhaul and realignment.

And, once changed, there was no going back. I had been cracked wide open!

After my morning meditation, I did some automatic writing and the following advice, which directly correlated with my time in the hospital, came through.

### DON'T GIVE YOUR POWER AWAY TO OTHERS

*"Always seek advice from your own Source of wisdom, not from others around you. It's good to have teachers and mentors, but you have all the tools already and you have a direct connection to all the answers that*

*are in your highest good. You don't need waste time or energy seeking answers from outside sources any longer.*

*You've been developing these skills your whole life and have been tapping into this inner knowing for years, even when you weren't consciously aware that's what it was. You're like the artist who's asked how long it took him to create his masterpiece. The answer is, his whole life!*

*You can tap into or connect with Source on a dime now... in an instant... you have already created that link and it's strong and growing stronger. We are here whenever you call upon us to remind you, guide you, support, and love you."*

I sat back and contemplated these words. Oftentimes, when people asked me what I do, I would call myself a "communication expert," which encompassed my twenty-plus years as a nationally certified Speech Language Pathologist and my work as a bridge between the spirit and physical worlds. While there were obvious dramatic differences, both involved the receiving, interpreting, and delivering of information to others. Clearly, though the speech pathology work I was doing was not my forever job and I would be moving out of it soon, it had given me skills that would be very useful in the future. No experience, knowledge, or skill would be wasted.

I also thought back to my teenage years, when I consciously began my spiritual journey in this lifetime. I would now be putting those skills and practices to use within a new framework and toward a much greater vision than I had ever imagined before.

## DAY FORTY-EIGHT

I slept much more soundly last night than I'd had in a while and awoke at 5:30 a.m. eager to start my day. Welcoming in the sun had become my morning ritual, and I looked out the sliding glass doors, taking in the acres of private land stretching far and wide against a backdrop of mountains and, of course, the beautiful Joshua trees reaching their branches like arms up to the heavens. I felt as though I could hear the heartbeat of the Earth. I sensed something so magical and holy, while at the same time grounding. No wonder, as, like Sedona, it is a powerful spiritual center with multiple energy vortices. I thought about the story behind the Joshua trees and the words repeatedly used to describe them: faith, survival, resilience. I could relate!

The melody and words from "The Wind" by Cat Stevens played in my mind, so I pulled it up on Spotify to enjoy while sipping coffee and soaking in the view. When I heard the first couple of lines, I was so moved I burst into tears. Stevens' lyrics about following one's soul and trusting in Spirit perfectly described what I was living and embodying right now.

After work today, I visited the Institute of Mental Physics, which was only a few minutes away from the house. At their bookstore, I was met by a very kind woman behind the counter who just so happened to have been born in Fort Bragg – the North Carolina Army base near where my parents still reside! Of all people, in all places! We had a lovely connection and I told her about my journey and that I'd been doing a lot of writing, photography and creative work, which I felt may end up in some kind of book format. She was so excited for me and said that when I finish my book to let her know so she can stock them in her store – and buy one for herself!

I then took a scenic drive through The Joshua Tree National Park. The scenery was amazing! The deeper I went into the park, the more "meditative" I felt, as if in a half-altered state. I was definitely feeling the vortex energy!

We don't necessarily have to be sitting in meditation to feel plugged in. Of course, this happens when I'm doing a mediumship or psychic reading, but it also happens when I am creating artistically – be it photography, sketching, playing piano, or writing. I am still receiving inspiration from the muses of the Universe. Same goes for when I'm hiking out in nature. I feel so alive and connected to the Earth energies and Elementals.

My affirmation:

**Every day it is my intention to be living my full purpose, the embodiment of my soul, and to have this show through in everything I think, feel, say, or do.**

## DAY FORTY-NINE

Today was my last full day here in Joshua Tree. Tomorrow I would make my way to Mount Shasta, and though I still wasn't sure about the route, I did feel called to follow the one the woman at the bookstore had recommended.

I did my own search last night but became so tired sifting through hotels and routes that I shut the computer down and went to bed without reserving anything. I woke from a dream with the message not to worry, that my team would guide me to the right path and hotel in the morning. I had not, however, been given any clarity on my direction and so woke up feeling off-center and wobbly.

I put out my energetic request for guidance to the Spirit world, and I started receiving as soon as I opened the first tab on my web browser. There were two possible paths I'd been contemplating: one heading toward Monterey and the other toward Lake Tahoe. I recalled the woman at the bookstore gushing over how beautiful the scenic drive was along 395 and saw that this would lead directly to Tahoe. That was my answer! Obviously, this was another reason I was guided to go to the bookstore. That was the breadcrumb and now I finally got the message.

**There's more than 1 way to get to the same destination. One is not necessarily better than another. Both will get you to where you want to go.**

**Sometimes, you just have to make a choice and take action and the rest will fall into place.**

CHAPTER EIGHT

# LIGHT

***"The light reminds you that because of its power nothing remains in the dark. Because of its illumination, truths and certain paths begin to emerge and can be surely seen."***

**~ John Holland**
**The Psychic Tarot Oracle Deck**

# DAY FIFTY-ONE

## Mt. Shasta, CA

I woke before my alarm again having had a good night's rest, ready and excited for a new day and a new place. I knew that while my personal healing would likely continue, I had already made a lot of progress in clearing and releasing. My sense was that this upcoming phase of my journey would focus on a deep dive into learning healing work I could offer to others.

Healing can happen in so many more ways than our human minds typically envision. I was reminded of the evening before, when I was waiting to pay for my dinner to go. I could tell that the young person behind the counter was feeling very awkward and was probably new to the job. He looked nervous and almost seemed to be physically shaking! At first, I was a little amused by his interaction with the gruff customer who was just in front of me in line. In the same instant, however, I realized that even as an observer I was affecting the outcome of this situation. Not wanting to contribute to someone else's discomfort, I immediately refocused and shifted my energy with the conscious intention to change the vibration of this environment and positively influence the people within it.

I visualized myself emanating light and love from my heart and silently sent positive, encouraging words to the young man behind the counter. A few minutes later, I was amazed and delighted to hear that same gruff customer, who at first appeared rather irritable, actually begin saying encouraging and complimentary comments to him!

I'd been consciously intending to be a positive **light** in the world and to offer uplifting energy and comfort wherever I went and everyone I met. I loved seeing the faces of strangers light up with a simple gesture, a smile, or a kind word. It's such a simple thing we can do to bring about positive changes to the people and world around us.

I arrived in Mount Shasta and got settled in the studio I'd rented, then drove five minutes into town – my first order of business: coffee. Then, with a steaming cup in hand, I strolled along the main strip. So fun to see so many alternative shops in one area, how amazing to have a breathtaking view of Mount Shasta from every street. It truly was, as the numerous signs read, *"Where Heaven and Earth Meet."*

## DAY FIFTY-TWO

This morning, after waking up to my alarm at 5:30 a.m., I started the coffee pot and then lay back down for a quick meditation while it brewed. I turned on the lights so I wouldn't fall back to sleep.

At first, I couldn't focus. My mind kept kicking in with worrisome thoughts about the money I was spending in my travels, conversations with family, what I was going to be doing the next leg of this journey, and so on. Finally, though, I was able to let go of the mind chatter and really drop into my meditation.

Afterward, while sipping my coffee, I did a quick check-in with my tarot cards. I set the intention to receive answers to the following: "What do I need to know today? What will help me the most right now on my path? You know," I added, "I could really use something uplifting, a little hope about where I'm headed."

I smiled – and teared up with love and appreciation – when I saw what appeared to be a quick and direct answer to my prayer. My first card,

**LIGHT,** depicted a woman reaching up her arms as if healed and uplifted by the source of that golden light.

Nearly two months into this journey, I still sometimes felt like I was in the dark, with no clear sense of direction. And, to be honest, my favorite times of the day was when I was in meditation or out of my body. I'd been having my up-and-down emotions all along the way. I wanted to feel confident that I was on the right path and that I was evolving and being purposeful, but I had doubts.

This message came when I needed reassurance that things would become clearer and the path would be lighted to show me the way. I just need to stay focused on the positive.

After completing my therapy sessions, I decided to walk into town to grab coffee and a snack, then come back to read and relax... maybe even take a nap. It was a very cold day, and on my way I stopped at my car to grab a winter coat. Yes, hot coffee was definitely needed!

A little while later, my coffee in hand, I was about to head back to the apartment when I felt a gentle nudge to get a reading at Soul Connections, a shop I had seen the day before. I walked in and asked if their tarot reader was available. If so, I added, it was meant to be; if not, that was fine too. Turned out she was just finishing up and could take me right away!

Her name was Margot. It was interesting to watch her work. She used traditional tarot cards and had a style very different from my own.

Some keys she highlighted from the reading:

The first card that she pulled for me: **HEALING.**

**SURRENDER** (to my path and to Spirit) was another theme that showed up early on in the reading. Margot said she saw this as a very positive card for me, indicating how tranquil and willing I now was to let go and surrender to my path.

She also passed on the advice to not give up my power to others and, furthermore, to not give up on my dreams because of past disappointments.

"You can throw away your training wheels," she said, adding that while more time was needed to be by myself, I didn't need any more dark nights of the soul. Couldn't agree more! In other words, self-healing and reflection is fine, but don't get caught up in revisiting, thinking about, or focusing on the past.

Finally, she pulled the QUEEN OF CUPS and said, "This is who you are!" She advised me to see myself as this beautiful, powerful queen and reiterated that I should not allow others to take away my power. "Don't settle for anyone or anything who doesn't rise up to meet you where you are. It's time to step into your power. You already have the strength, power, and tools within you to reach enlightenment."

As the session was coming to a close, she peered out the window and exclaimed, "Do you see that? Is that money?!" She ran outside and grabbed a ten-dollar-bill that was floating by. What an excellent sign for us both! She took it as a "tip" from Spirit, buying me some extra time for my reading. In fact, she actually took quite a bit of extra time, continuing to give me guidance and encouragement. It was so generous of her and obviously Spirit-led. I knew they had arranged it all and were giving me loving encouragement through this receptive channel.

## DAY FIFTY-THREE

Last night I had set my alarm for 4:44 a.m., which would give me just enough time to quickly wash my face, make some coffee, and be online for a five o'clock Spiritualist Healing Class. As tired as I was, I was so glad I attended. It felt so good to be in this group and doing such purposeful work. Whenever I did art and channeled healing, it felt so natural, as if I was doing the work I was meant to be doing. I felt like I was home.

The class was followed by an easy morning of online therapy sessions and really enjoyable connections with my students. My little kindergarteners smiled and laughed the whole time, and one of them even gave me a virtual hug by embracing her computer! My middle-schooler was so playful and silly, making the speech aid and me laugh so hard our cheeks hurt. It was lovely! This is the kind of influence and energy I always wanted to share and co-create with people. It didn't even feel like work.

Later that day, I headed into town, excited about my appointment at Starlight Healing Arts. The owner and healer, Oksana Zavoyko, was going to do an "Arcturian Healing," and I was intrigued as to what it entailed, especially since I kept getting messages in my meditations about my connection with the Arcturians.

As Oksana got started with the grounding process, I was able to stay present and immediately felt a strong presence creating sparks of electrical impulses over my body. Minutes later, however, I dove into a very deep state, completely unconscious of the outside world. About halfway through the healing session, I landed back in my body with a gasp of air while still remaining in a deeply connected state. Next thing I knew, I was out again, traveling swiftly through a tunnel of golden sparkling light. At the end of the tunnel, I came face to face with a being who looked just like myself, radiating light and smiling at me. I began seeing and feeling codes being downloaded and streamed directly into my head and down into body, spiraling around and integrating with my DNA! Someone or something communicated that I would be able to access and understand this information as it unfolded along my path in a future time.

When the session was complete and I was firmly back in my physical body, Oksana poured me a hot cup of tea while we sat and compared notes on what we had experienced.

Oksana said that the energy during the healing was very intense and powerful, and I confirmed that I had felt it too! She initially sensed the presence of Archangel Metatron and said it was unusual for him to come forward during her sessions. He had come to empower me and remained present the entire time to guide and assist us. She suggested calling upon him in my meditations, but added that there were actually a total of eight Guides or Angels working with me.

Oksana continued describing her experience, but when she mentioned an interstellar portal, I gasped out loud. Not only had I traveled through a tunnel – or portal – during the healing, I had been receiving the word "interstellar" a lot in my meditations! She'd also received information that I had incarnated multiple times as different types of beings, but was especially being assisted by Arcturians and Archangels now. I didn't doubt it for a minute; in fact, just that morning in my meditation I had received a download that synced up with what Oksana was talking about now. It was incredibly validating.

I asked her about the purpose of connecting with these different entities. She explained that understanding our origin, our incarnations, or associations helps us better understand and tap into the unique qualities and skills we are meant to use in this life.

"You have the ability to positively and powerfully influence others through your presence, your energy, without having to even speak."

Funny – Michael had said the same thing during the psychic reading he gave me before I began this whole adventure.

"You can change and raise the vibrational energy of people just through your intention," Oksana added.

This was exactly what I'd been guided to do! So far, it was all making sense and enlightening me even further on things that had been coming up for me recently.

She told me that during my healing session she had tapped into my Akashic records and helped clear any lingering sense of lack or separation within in order to open me up and accelerate me on my path. You're already well-attuned to the fifth dimension, but now your intention should be focused on completely merging with this vibration, being in total harmony with it... living and embodying this energy in every moment.

As our time came to a close, I gave her a huge hug and many thanks. She teared up a little, saying she could see that I would be doing much good in the world, and how much she loved being in my presence because my energy was so pure, innocent – almost childlike – and uplifting. What a blessing to meet another lightworker and connect in such a beautiful way!

Before I left, Oksana asked where I was headed next. I candidly replied that I didn't know yet but was contemplating somewhere a bit more south. She then mentioned Harbin Hot Springs, which I'd never heard of (only locals really know about it) until the night before, when I "happened" to be looking at it on a map! Right after she started telling me about it, I saw a bright golden and white light spark above her head, like a wink from the Universe. I would be booking a reservation at Harbin Hot Springs soon.

## DAY FIFTY-FIVE

Fifty-five is a powerful number symbolizing CHANGE, TRANSFORMATION, so this day felt especially significant. I had booked my next rental in Lake Port, close to Harbin Hot Springs, and was curious to check out this place Oksana had raved about. I was also so grateful to have received a recommendation for a place that offered a different type of healing.

Last night a dream revealed some stagnant energy surrounding my sexuality and past experiences that had made me feel disconnected and disempowered. These had not only negatively impacted my intimate relationships but also my relationship with myself.

I documented the dream, then prayed for help in releasing any remaining blocked energy surrounding the rape and any other negative sexual experience I may still be holding onto. Then, I closed my eyes and laid back down in bed, opening myself up to divine healing energy. As soon as my body and mind settled, I saw a team of light beings form around me. I felt their energy and could hear a buzz around me. I heard my name called, as if the speaker was right there in the room, then felt tingling in different areas of my body as they worked on me. It was so comforting and loving, and I just surrendered to any assistance coming my way.

## DAY FIFTY-SIX

My last night in Mount Shasta was going to be a FULL FLOWER MOON with a partial lunar eclipse. A quick Google search revealed that the sun, earth, and moon were not quite in alignment with each other yet. Hmm, I thought, sounds like me!

Determined to make the most of the rest of my stay, I headed out on a hike. I felt the need to get grounded and reconnect with the healing energy of nature and, thankfully, the weather complied.

When I returned to the apartment, I laughed aloud at what I had left on my dining/work table. Apparently, these were my must-haves for my solo soul journey:

1 Fully-Charged Laptop and solid Wi-Fi
Multiple Tarot and Oracle Decks

1 Bundle of Sage
1 Stack of Inspiring Metaphysical Books
2 Crystal Necklaces

And… of course…

1 Fully-Charged Vibrator

## CRYSTAL BOWL SOUND HEALING

This evening, I had a wonderful experience in a small group sound healing. I arrived a little early and was able to talk with Donna, the woman conducting the healing, and another participant, Richard, who had lived in Mount Shasta for over thirty years. He said there was a potent, very inspiring creative energy here, then asked if I write because I could tap into this energy. I could always use extra inspiration with my creative projects and ideas!

Once the sounds started, I felt different chakras opening and moving. My body was vibrating all over, starting in my crown before spilling down through my arms and hands. My throat chakra became activated, and the words "Clearing, Allow, Let Go, Awakening, Activating" flowed repeatedly through my mind. I sensed that the sound vibrations functioned almost like mantras for our bodies, attuning us to higher vibrations. Even with the last lingering vibrations of her bowls, my heart chakra was still spinning, my whole body still vibrating, and all of my senses fully awakened! What a fantastic way to end my final day here.

I was so thankful for the time and access to try these different types of healings over the past week. It is especially important for those doing healing work to incorporate a regular practice of healing for ourselves to keep our energy and channels clear.

CHAPTER NINE

# TRANSFORMATION

***"The death of an old way of thinking and believing must occur before you can move forward on your path… opportunity will come to expand you in more ways than you could have ever imagined."***

**~ John Holland**
**The Psychic Tarot Oracle Deck**

# DAY FIFTY-EIGHT

## Mount Shasta to Lake Port, CA

I woke to my alarm at 5:30 a.m. and said a quick thank you for a new day. In thirty minutes, I would attend an online healing workshop with a new teacher, which I was very excited about. Whenever I'm channeling healing energy, it feels amazing, like I'm doing the work I came here to do.

The instructor for the healing workshop was definitely speaking my language:

> ***"Before you can be artists within healing, you have to give yourself and the Spirit world time so your own body and soul can heal. The body needs food, the brain needs knowledge, and our souls needs love."***
>
> ~Danielle Nijhuis

For healing mediumship, we have to have already logged quite a bit of time sitting and communing with the Spirit world to establish and sustain a solid connection. I'd had a dedicated meditation practice before, but it'd deepened to a whole other level since I'd been on this journey. Aside from my speech therapy sessions and traveling from one location to another, my time and energy had been devoted to my own development, awareness, and connection to Spirit. As a result, my relationship with myself and with the Divine had become so much more intimate.

The workshop marked the end of my stay in Mount Shasta. I finished packing, then went about doing some last-minute cleaning and straightening up. It made me think of the private message I'd received from the owner of the home where I'd stayed in Joshua Tree: *"It's such a rare thing to see a guest care for our space as mindfully and respectfully as you did. You are welcome back anytime."* Wherever I am or whomever I'm with, I want to leave them better than they were before. That is my intention and the kind of energy I want to bring.

When I was ready to leave I glanced at my phone and saw it was 10:10 – an angel number signifying endings leading to new beginnings and awakening to one's life purpose. Bring it on!

As much as I'd enjoyed being here for the last week, I needed to stretch my wings and try something new. Each place I visited was like another chamber in the nautilus shell. The more I grew and expanded, the more I needed to allow more space, with each new experience building on the previous one.

I slid behind the wheel, giving thanks for the mild weather. It was rainy, but it hadn't snowed last night or this morning as had been forecasted. I then sent out an asking to please surround my car and me with protection and grant us easy travels all the way to my next destination. I also thanked my car for being such a rockstar as it carried me these incredibly long distances, in all kinds of weather, and across all kinds of terrains with me.

Along the way, I passed a truck with the slogan, ***"Helping the world deliver on their promises."*** Yes! That's what I want to do, starting with myself and hopefully inspiring others to do the same.

I started thinking about people like me – freedom-seekers longing for soul connection – and how I might inspire them to embark on their own soul trip. I imagined an online community which could serve as a support network, offering connection and encouragement for one another along the way.

Each individual's journey would look different because we are all such unique souls, starting from different places and with varying innate talents needing expression. Since I happened to be opening up my psychic, mediumistic, and healing skills, I'd been drawn, by design, to people and places who will help me fulfill my soul's plan. We are each here to discover and embrace our own exceptional nature. Anyone who steps onto this path is voluntarily choosing to participate in an extended exercise in trusting their intuition.

My original plan when I arrived in Lake Port was to go for a run and enjoy the day outdoors, but I just didn't feel up for that. The path I had chosen at times felt overwhelming and emotionally draining – and I had learned to recognize when I just needed to pause, rest, and reset. When I saw a place offering reflexology and massage, I didn't hesitate.

It was wonderful. When the gentleman started working on my feet, I felt energy being channeled in by my spirit healers. Even when he briefly stepped out to get some new towels, it felt as though my feet were still being massaged and energy was flowing from my head right to my toes. I saw that the masseuse had a little cough he was trying to suppress and I couldn't help but to put out the intention for Spirit to channel healing energy through me to him as well. Always called to the healing work!

That evening in my meditation, I was told by my team to just relax and rest my mind and body. My mind had so many thoughts running through it – more than "normal" – and I spent the first several minutes releasing them. I was assured that I was doing more than enough and all I needed right now was to rest.

The words "Star Being" popped into my mind and my guides explained that it was my nature to want to focus the intense energy I was always carrying inside of me; Michael, the psychic, had said it was "like someone put a jet engine into a Volkswagen." Harnessing and purposely directing this energy was part of my plan and my purpose, so that's why not having a clear direction or plan always felt very uncomfortable to me.

I was always trying to find that balance between doing and resting, receiving inspiration and taking inspired action... it's like a dance. I knew I'd been giving without allowing receiving and replenishing and was out of balance. Time to restore.

Before bed, I pulled one tarot card: **TRANSFORMATION**

I closed my eyes and tapped into my own inner guidance regarding this card and received the following in my automatic writing:

***This is a time of major transformation for you. It's hard to see it when you're the one in the middle of it and we know it's not always easy, but know that you are still in gestation right now – in the cocoon. so to speak – and soon will emerge as a beautiful butterfly.***

***Of course, your growth and expansion never ends, but this current time of isolation will be coming to an end soon.***

***Be patient with this time of growth as it's building a solid foundation for you that will carry you far. Allow yourself more time on this very important journey leading you toward your soul's purpose.***

***Remember that it takes time and patience.***
***Allow the unfolding of who you are becoming.... the real you.***
***Who you came here to be.***

**Note: I pulled the same card again the next day!

## DAY SIXTY

I woke at 4:30 a.m., my new norm, with the phrase **"seeds of thought"** and the word **"untethered"** in my mind. As I sat down to document the dreams and downloads I had received during the night, I thought that untethered was a good way to describe how I felt... like a balloon set free by the wind with no strings attached. I was reminded I'd gotten rid of almost all my possessions – for the second time in the past five years – and was now living out of my suitcase, moving closer each day toward some unknown destination. Free. Untethered.

## Dream Sequence

I see my family (mom, dad, sister).

My mom says, "Happy birthday!"

I say, "It's not my birthday."

"It's not?" she asks.

I look at the date and I realize my birthday has already passed. It's now June twenty-first.

"Oh well," I say, "I guess we're celebrating a little late. I'm ready for some rest!"

My mom says something about putting my sneakers away.

We're near a bathroom and I suggest we move away from it for our celebration.

## Dream Interpretation

I knew the dream had to do with this adventure and believed it gave me specific information or advice on when it would end (June twenty-first, after my birthday). This would be when the clearing was done, as symbolized by the bathroom, and I could then go "home" and take off my shoes, for rest and celebration!

I'd never had a premonition with an exact date, so I considered this to be significant. When I looked at the calendar and calculated the days to get to this date, I saw that there were exactly twenty-one days left in this month, plus twenty-one days for the next month. Whoa! Again, I don't believe in coincidences and cannot ignore the June twenty-first date, followed by repeating twenty-ones.

I quickly looked up the meaning of **"2121"** and gasped when I saw the exact wording I was given in my dream:

*"The number* ***2121*** *indicates that your* ***thoughts are like seeds*** *that are about to sprout and are a sign that things will be going in your desired direction."*

From there, it was down the rabbit hole! I added up twenty-one and twenty-one, then googled the significance of the number forty-two. The first thing that popped up was that it was ***"The Answer to the Ultimate question of Life, the Universe, and Everything."***

This was a quote from *The Hitchhiker's Guide to the Galaxy,* the humorous sci-fi classic in which a supercomputer named "Deep Thought" offers "42" as the ultimate answer. The problem is that no one really knows what the question is.

Interestingly, I had just recently been listening to an audio that talked about "asking the right questions in order to get the right solutions," which is what happens in the film.

Just the night before, even my fortune cookie said, "You know all the answers but you're not asking the right questions." Clearly, I was being nudged to adjust my queries about life, and this journey in particular, in order to start accessing the information at my fingertips.

Well, I certainly didn't anticipate that I'd have the answer to the "ultimate question" of the Universe by June twenty-first – perhaps not even in this lifetime, but I did believe I would gain a greater sense of clarity for myself and my own path.

# DAY SIXTY-ONE

I loved the unique ways my spirit team worked with me and guided me – and last night was one of the most interesting yet. They gave me a tarot reading in my dream! As mentioned, dreams had always been a clear way to receive guidance, and I'd regularly documented and interpreted them since my teens. Lucid dreams were commonplace as well, and I'd even been given direct interpretation of my dreams *within* dreams before, but never had I had a tarot reading in a dream... until now.

### Dream Tarot: Three-Card Spread

My team had done a three-card spread, which I clearly recalled upon waking. When I connected with my guides and asked for their interpretation, I received the following:

**CARD #1 - Picture of Me.** "Despondent" was the word that came up first, an indicator of how I was feeling (i.e., in low spirits from a loss of hope or courage). The advice was contained within the lyrics to a song I had actually listened to recently: "Let It Go By."

**CARD #2 – Picture of a Knight Looking Right (toward the third card).** The knight indicated my incoming love/soulmate who was watching over me and patiently waiting for me.

**CARD #3 – Picture of Me Looking Left (toward the Knight).** The message: "Be patient and allow your own healing right now. It's not time yet, but don't give up on love because that's part of your path too."

I had a great psychic mediumship mentoring session this morning, which I was able to schedule at the last minute. It was so nice to have someone to open up to about everything I was experiencing on my journey and in my life. This teacher had read for me in our last psychic group, as part of a demonstration-style reading for the other participants to witness, and had brought forth very accurate information on my behalf.

During this morning's session, she added to that guidance and reminded me that all my "sacrifices" would pay off.

Psychic and mediumship readings are so intimate, as you open your heart and invite another person in to "see" things that are usually kept hidden from others.

She remarked, "You know, it's funny. People would have no idea about all you're going through now or ever guess that you have previously experienced such hardships across your life because you present yourself as such a put-together, happy, and confident person. No one would ever realize the true internal turmoil!"

Anyone reading this will see that I have had (and continue to have) lots of inner struggles. But I'm also very resilient and have come to know and trust that these struggles are temporary and I'll always get through them – with assistance, of course. As I was typing this, Spotify randomly started playing "Let it Go By" by Fiora – the Spirit-inspired soundtrack of my experience. I felt as if Spirit was sending a confirmation, like, "Yes, you are resilient and you will get through any challenge you are faced with. Trust and know that we've always got your back!"

I then received the download for my next destination: Klamath Falls, Oregon, near Crater Lake. I had wanted to visit there while in Mount Shasta but didn't end up going due to the wintry weather. Now that the weather was looking warmer and clearer, I was called to head north again.

Always feels good to make and act on a decision. It's the indecision and confusion that feels uncomfortable, though this venture is giving me lots of practice with this . . . daily!

# DAY SIXTY-THREE

This morning, I was pondering a question that I've been asked by clients: "Why are we born into this life with no memory of who/what we really are or were in past incarnations?"

Well, if you already knew every possible outcome in advance, what'd be the point of incarnating here at all? You didn't come here to simply follow a script, say your lines as they're written. You came to be part of the creation process and write the script as you go.

This reminds me of when I practice conversational skills with my students with autism. We start with scripted practice in the learning process, but to achieve mastery they have to be able to spontaneously lead and participate on a variety of topics with different situations and people without the lines in front of them.

Another great analogy is comparing our life experience to an improvisational comedy. We have general guidelines and set up some situations, but if we knew everything in advance how boring and pointless would it be? Not only would we miss out on the opportunity to learn and therefore expand or grow, it just wouldn't be as much fun or interesting. It's the element of surprise, something unexpected or unplanned, unscripted, that brings the most enjoyment.

The great thing is that here, we DO have lots of support along the way. We *always* have a team waiting and watching in the wings who are there offering nudges, guidance, and clues and giving us lines at key moments when we're lost or unsure. We aren't left to figure it all out on our own. We are actually in this shared Universal classroom with teachers, healers, and helpers who love us and are always cheering us on and helping us whenever they can. All we need to do is ask and listen.

## HARBIN HOT SPRINGS

While I was up in Mount Shasta, two different people recommended I visit Harbin Hot, a spa retreat center. I had to check out this local favorite; in fact, it was the reason I'd decided to stay in Lake Port, one of the closest towns with available rentals. It was actually one of the oldest hot springs in California and considered a sacred healing place for the region's Native people.

Before I knew it, I was soaking in the healing waters of their historic silent meditation pool. It was pretty crowded, but so nice to just close my eyes and float in the water among the community of individuals all looking for some inner peace, just as I was. It was also very liberating, considering it's a clothing-optional place and pretty much everyone opted out!

Once I'd had enough sunning and soaking, I headed over to a Qigong class taught by a woman named Asha. She had such a sweet, gentle, almost fragile nature about her; she was also very present, heartfelt, and genuine. I found the flow of movements very meditative, beautifully connecting and balancing the energies of the spiritual and physical worlds.

After class, I stopped by their nearby cafe to grab a smoothie for the road. While standing in line, the man in front of me started up a conversation. A former professor for a graduate program in genetics, he was now a fellow nomad going wherever he felt inspired to go. He told me he'd be coming to Harbin Hot since he was in his early twenties, then laughed, saying, "It seems like I'm too weird for most people and places!"

*Like attracts like,* I thought. We "weirdos" tend to naturally gravitate toward one another.

Asha joined us, and we had a fun conversation about Qigong, meditation, alternative healing, my psychic mediumship work, and more. I was getting so pumped up with ideas as I talked about my future aspirations that my new friends commented excitedly that my "rockstar energy" was recharging their batteries too! Both were also eager to set up sessions with me.

It was an awesome way to end the visit to Harbin, topped off with 4:44 on the clock when I got in the car. As I headed "home," it hit me that THIS connection was a big reason why I was guided to come here.

That evening, for the third time that week, the TRANSFORMATION card showed up again for me!

## DAY SIXTY-FOUR

*" Your soul self knows the journey.*
*It knows the way.*
*Allow the unfoldment."*

~ Pam Meredith

I had truly been enjoying exploring all the different cities on this trip, yet I hadn't felt a strong enough connection to want to live in any of these places. The real connection, I realized, was to the various people I'd met along the way. Everywhere I went, I had made some beautiful connection, be it a fellow yoga student, a healer, psychic medium, or wanderer; sometimes it was a hitchhiker I met along the road. I knew I was being placed in the presence of specific people so I could offer and receive some inspiration, rejuvenation, healing, encouragement, and connection in a magical exchange. Though they appeared to be strangers, they were in fact my fellow Starseeds.

My life was transforming and unfolding like the thousand- petaled lotus, one petal at a time, one experience at a time. And yet I knew that the number of petals was infinite, with no end to the unfolding. I was creating the life I really wanted and drawing on so many adventures, not just on this road but in the past as well. I had traveled all over the world and undertaken what many would think were risky activities – ridden a motorcycle across South Africa; climbed Kilimanjaro one and a half times (that's a whole other story), hiked the Inca Trail to Machu Picchu, and on and on... Looking back, I could honestly say I had no regrets, and I was far from done. I was living fully, experiencing the full range life has to offer. And I brought each and every life experience with me into my readings, my teachings, and my interactions with people. For this, I would always be grateful.

## Crystal Sound Healing

On my final day in Lake Port, I treated myself to a wonderful crystal sound healing session. When I arrived, Laurel, the healer and owner of the practice, sensed that my chakras were all clear but my solar plexus, third eye, and crown chakras were wide open and spinning like helicopters in need of balance.

I don't usually deal much with past lives, so it was interesting when Laurel passed on a message from my guides about karma from previous incarnations. Then, as she worked on me, this message dropped into my mind: ***"Release your fear of persecution and judgment that you've carried from past lives and allow yourself to step into the public eye more; allow yourself to come out as the psychic medium and healer that you are."***

I felt so relaxed, grounded, and balanced after the session and ended up making another great connection with Laurel, who ironically used to live in the same Raleigh zip code as me! When I told her that I was indeed doing psychic mediumship and spiritual healing work, just as she had sensed, she immediately requested a session with me. More divine orchestration!

CHAPTER TEN

# SPIRITUAL STRENGTH

***"Courage, discipline, stability, and persistence… You've been through so much to get to this point; and even though you may have acquired some scars from the battle, you're wiser and stronger for it."***

**~ John Holland**
**The Psychic Tarot Oracle Deck**

# DAY SIXTY-FIVE

## Klamath Falls, OR

I left early, heading north to Oregon. As I drove, I recalled with gratitude all the beautiful synchronistic meetings I'd had – several of which resulted in requests for readings from me. And yet, I realized, I still felt some hesitation to fully put myself out there as a psychic medium… Why?

So funny that not a minute after mentally asking the question, I saw a sign that said ***"Got questions? God has answers!"*** Then, as promised, I received divine clarity on the answer:

*You already know why you're hesitant. It's a lack of self-confidence.*
*Have confidence in yourself. And if that's still difficult for you,*
*at least have confidence in US.*
*Trust in us that we will not let you down and we will always come*
*through. We will always support you, but YOU have to take the step.*

I arrived in good time at the new place, a sweet rental space designed as a speakeasy. All midcentury modern retro with some steampunk accents, it was very cool and spacious, with lots of seating and a whole wall of window space for natural lighting. However, as usual, I felt a little off having landed in an unfamiliar setting and needed to ground myself.

Though I love to travel and am much more flexible than the average person, these weekly moves were proving a challenge to my sense of balance. No doubt about it, this trip was giving me lots of practice in testing my ability to adjust quickly to new situations and attune myself to new environments.

## DAY SIXTY-SIX

Insights upon waking had been coming with greater regularity. This morning, I had the thought that one reason I sometimes cried for no reason was that I was taking on the energy of people around me. Of course, I was also still in the process of my own clearing, releasing any obstacles that came in the form of self-doubt, judgment, lack of self-confidence, worry, et cetera. It was a two-fold process.

I then realized that each place I was led to caused an internal shift, shaking up the old paradigm within me and allowing me to release and transmute any remaining patterns so I could come into harmony and stabilization. I was sensitive to and affected by the energy of each place, including the neighborhoods, members of the various households, energetic imprint from the last guests, and even the land and surrounding environment. I always knew it was no coincidence (after all, nothing is!) that I was being guided to powerful spiritual centers and vortex areas. But I was now being given clarity as to why:

> **The intense energy of these sacred areas were creating much bigger shifts within me, and moving the clearing and awakening process along at a much more rapid rate than would happen anywhere else.**

Much more surprising was the understanding that a beautiful synergy was happening. As I conducted my spiritual practice with the conscious intention to leave each space better than I'd found it, I not only realigned *myself* further but helped *to raise the vibration of the place and people around me.* The more I allowed myself to receive and realign, the more I had to give back. The more I released and opened up to being a clearer channel, the more could flow through me to share with the world. **Healing myself helped heal the people and places around me.**

The message that I needed to allow more balance on the receiving end came up during my psychic development circle later that morning. During our reading exchange my partner pulled the **Spiritual Strength** card from The Psychic Tarot deck for me. I needed to ask and let others help me more, she said, adding:

> *"Allow someone else to help bear the weight for you instead of trying to do it alone. Know that you don't walk alone, but walk hand in hand."*

## DAY SIXTY-SEVEN

I had originally planned to drive to Crater Lake today, but just wasn't feeling it. The roads were probably safe, but I kept getting the nudge that I could instead go all day Friday since all of my speech pathology sessions had been canceled. Plus, the weather would be warmer.

I was so appreciative for my clients, for a steady stream of income, as well as the flexibility of a virtual job, which allowed me the freedom to travel as I was. At the same time, I had been ready to transition out of speech therapy for several years and was burned out. I just didn't know exactly what my new career would entail or how I'd make the leap since my formal education had all been related to communication. Still, I always had the desire to move in a new direction that would allow me to fully embrace and share the gifts within my spiritual wheelhouse. I had been unclear on the details of what I'd be offering to the world, but was now finally seeing this coming to light. It was actually a very natural progression of moving from my career as a communication expert for the physical world to now stepping into the role as a communication expert working with the spirit world. I'd always worked so hard to keep the two worlds separate, but now I understood that the bridge was already built to connect these two worlds. In actuality, I WAS the bridge. With one foot on each side, I was to serve as a communicator, an interpreter, and teacher for the wisdom, guidance, love, and focused activating and healing energy from "the other side."

Thankfully, I also had a cancellation today, which gave me a much-needed break between sessions. I was exhausted, but took the time to do a meditation. I was shown a vision of myself under my car hood, checking the oil reading on the stick.

After my last session, I decided to hike a trail by Klamath Lake that I'd read about and thought looked good. Recalling my meditation, I figured I should probably stop and check my oil first, just in case. Turns out the oil was so low it barely showed on the stick, even though it had been topped off a couple cities earlier! There was a quick oil change place just five minutes away, and they were able to take care of everything for me no problem. Yay! Thank God for this guidance to check my oil and to postpone my drive to Crater Lake! The Universe always has my back, that's for sure.

I headed out to find the trail, but when I got there the directions weren't as clear as they seemed when I researched it (and, of course, there was no signage.) I politely asked for directions from a man who looked like a resident of the area and he was able to at least point me in the right direction. One path led to another and before I knew it I was on the trail.

**Just get started and you will be guided to exactly where you need to go.**

Until then, I had been busy with sessions, getting my car serviced, and finding the trail. Once I settled into my hike, however, I felt some emotions start to come up. I realized I needed grounding. I was uneasy and a bit lonely; I just hadn't connected with this town or its people yet. I allowed myself to feel the emotions and then set an intention to release them for transmutation and clearing from every cell in my body. As I walked, I took, long deep breaths in and out and used the go-to walking meditation mantra I'd created for myself a while back for releasing and alchemizing all misaligned and unwanted energies:

**Breathing in… CLARITY**
**Breathing out…uncertainty**
**Breathing in…. LOVE**
**Breathing out…fear**
**Breathing in… PEACE**
**Breathing out…discomfort**

A little further down the trail, I encountered a woman and her sweet dog. She smiled warmly and greeted me as if we were long lost friends, exclaiming, "Did you see the egrets?! They're nesting all over the trail! I've been walking this trail for years and I've never seen them nest here! It's amazing!" She pointed me to the spot where I could see them. I thanked her for the tip, though I didn't actually know what "egrets" were and I was curious and eager to see what the excitement was about.

I continued on my way and soon heard the egrets' sound; then, I suddenly saw hundreds of these elegant white crane-like birds sitting in the trees and a few flying above. It truly was an incredible sight, and I suddenly felt inspired to look them up.

As it turned out, egrets symbolized exactly how I was feeling: uneasy, uncertain, alone. They were said to present themselves to "those who find themselves in between places, people, or phases in their life." How about all three for me! I had a long- term lease in this liminal space and this graceful spirit animal was a spiritual sign offering comfort through the transformation process. Clearly, Spirit had enlisted this kind woman to deliver the message, timed perfectly with the appearance of these birds.

No matter how many times I experienced synchronicities of the Universe, I never ceased to be amazed!

While meditating in the late afternoon, I was shown three tarot cards in my mind's eye and told that my team would work with me in this way more and more (i.e., showing me the tarot cards in my mind, rather than my having to pull physical cards).

The first card, from Radleigh Valentine's Angel Wisdom Tarot Deck, depicted a man by a stream with five cups, three overturned and broken, before him. He was so focused on the empty cups that he didn't notice the two other, full cups being handed to him. The card was coming to show that no matter how things my appear right now, I needn't worry about money or abundance because it was coming very soon just around the corner, in fact. The Angels had my back.

I was next shown a Spirit-inspired tarot card with an image of a woman being seen through a magnifying glass and looking very unhappy about the pressure the world was putting upon her. This obviously represented me and the unnecessary worry and stress I was feeling about everything.

Last, I was again shown the Spiritual Strength card from The Psychic Tarot and told to let my team take the weight of the world off of my shoulders. The takeaway message here was:

***Just continue to walk your path and we will carry the weight.***

## DAY SIXTY-EIGHT

I was guided to the perfect video this morning about the spiritual awakening process and how it involves a complete shift of our central nervous system and energetic frequencies. It was comforting to be reminded that these changes are accompanied by emotional and physical release in the form of uneasiness, sadness, exhaustion, or crying for no reason. This is part of the clearing process, so I could stop judging myself for feeling this way and just allow this process to continue since it was actually a positive sign of growth and expansion.

In fact, when I thought about it, I could say I'd been pretty stable and grounded, considering that I'd just gone through a huge shift in all areas of my life: romantic relationships, friendships, location, home, and work – not to mention a much deeper spiritual awakening.

In a mentoring session this morning, my teacher, Pam, reminded me of my recent demonstration of mediumship (or "platform mediumship," where mediums connect with a "communicator," or spirit person, and find their loved one in the audience). I had gotten a double link with a fellow medium in order to give messages for our sitter. Pam was so impressed with this, and with the entire group, saying that if we weren't already doing so we should all be offering readings outside our circle; she would easily pay money, she added, for a reading like the one I had done. It was really nice to have this vote of confidence from my mentor and another hand on my back, gently pushing me further out of the spiritual closet.

I also appreciated Pam's advice on determining when we're ready to move from practice to professional work. She explained that we're still human and that the information we're receiving must cross time and space consciousness! If we're eighty percent accurate eighty percent of the time, that's great! It was the exact same thing I always explained to my speech therapy clients and families. **Perfection is not the barometer for mastery; they are not synonymous.** When people are striving for perfection, they are often unwilling to take risks because it could involve failure and disappointment. This applied to every goal in life; I recalled Jared's daughter refusing to learn a musical instrument. She wouldn't be able to quickly and easily master it, she said, so why bother trying? She had completely missed the point of trying something new, which was for the experience and the fun of the journey, not the destination.

Validation also came from Angie, another regular mentor and a teacher at Arthur Findlay College (considered to be the "Hogwarts" of mediumship.) In my reading for her during our last meeting, I had described Angie's move to her ideal home with her romantic partner. This move, which would happen very soon, would be to a sacred area surrounded by nature; her soul would feel at home there. Thanking me, Angie announced that, that exact thing had happened within the same week! I knew Spirit was behind these confidence boosters and I greatly appreciated it!

Tonight, I relaxed and watched a show with dinner; then I popped open the craft beer the owners had left for me and looked for inspiration on where I would head next. I felt blocked, unsure of my direction. I also had another solid week of therapy sessions, which limited when/where I could travel at a time... hence the week-at-a-time stays. Finally, I settled on nearby town of Bend, Oregon, which would allow me to further explore the state a bit before moving on.

**Sometimes, just making a decision, even one you're not completely sure of, feels good.**

## DAY SEVENTY

This morning, I listened to an interview with Andy Byng, another psychic medium with roots at Arthur Findlay. He reminded me that while most people focus all their efforts on improving the technical aspects of their mediumship, the majority of our time and energy would be better spent on self-development. That, he said, is how we truly improve our ability to connect with the Spirit world.

*"Emotion is at the center of the whole communication process. Mediumship is about mastering the self. To master mediumship is to master oneself."*

**~ Andy Byng**

For so many years, I had been focused on self-development; that was why I was able to open up my psychic and mediumship skills. However, it wasn't until much later in life (and through some serious a-ha moments) that I'd finally begun to realize my potential.

A few years back, I'd gone to Sedona for some me time and rejuvenation. A "Celebrate Your Life" event had happened the week before, but there were some post-conference workshops that coincided with my trip. I'd never heard of the instructor, Sunny Dawn Johnston, but liked the sound of her intuition workshop. In addition to her teaching, she did a telepathy exercise in which she'd hold up different cards, turned away from us, and ask us to call out what they were. Everyone was doing pretty poorly, and we all laughed and joked, "Well, I guess we're not psychic!" When we quieted, Sunny asked what our process was for tapping into our guidance. We all looked a little confused, trying to think back and figure out what we had done besides flat-out guessing. Then Sunny posed the question that made the lightbulb start flashing in my mind: "Well, did you ask your guides and angels to help you?"

A-ha! No, we hadn't!

Next time around, she pulled out her Multi-Dimensional Oracle deck and had each of us choose a card without looking at it. We then partnered up; the card we'd each pulled was meant for our partner. Before looking at the card, she instructed us to psychically tap in and receive a message about the card for the other person. This time, I closed my eyes and held the card to my heart, then set the intention and silently asked any angels and guides, "What does she need to know? Please show me what's on this card that I can share in her messaging." Suddenly, in my mind's eye I saw an image of a beautiful woman with dark hair surrounded by golden light. She was holding out her hands and in the middle of her hands was a light. It appeared that she was in nature with beautiful flowers and mountains. I jotted down the messages I was receiving and shared them with my partner.

When it was time to flip over the card, we both gasped in awe. The exact image I had seen in my mind's eye and had described for my partner was illustrated clearly on the oracle card! Furthermore, the messages aligned with the image. It was an aha-moment and wake-up call that I indeed had psychic abilities and was able to tap into messages from the Spirit world through my focus, intention, and asking.

After this experience, I signed up for mentorship with international medium Michelle Armstrong. We started with a get-to-know-you session during which she would read my energy. I remembered her saying that when she meets with students, she can sense their skill level right away; for most, it seemed like a drop in a bucket in terms of psychic or mediumship potential. Then she added, *"But when I tap into you, it's like tapping into the whole ocean when it comes to your power and potential."*

This made complete sense to me. For a while I'd been feeling as if I had all this dormant power within me, just waiting to be expressed. It was the reason I'd felt the push to pursue some training and mentorship.

One thing led to another, and before I knew it I was taking regular classes through both Arthur Findlay and Journey Within, which was where I'd met my current mentor, Pam Meredith. In fact, another huge a-ha moment happened during our first one-on-one mentoring session. Pam had me make a spirit connection for her so that she could see how I work. Being put on the spot this way was very nerve-wracking, but I reminded myself that this was exactly what I'd signed up for.

Closing my eyes, I took some deep breaths to calm myself, hoping and praying something would come through. Right away, I could see and sense a spirit and felt it could be Janet Nohavec, an extremely gifted medium, Spiritualist minister, and founder of the Journey Within. Recently, we had received the sad news that Janet, who was Pam's own mentor and dear friend, had passed away.

I immediately thought to myself, *"You're making this up. This is part of your mental projection."* However, Janet wasn't going away. I then actually had the balls to politely ask the great Janet Nohavec to please step aside for now because it wasn't good timing and I didn't think Pam was going to believe me...I mean, *I* didn't even believe me at this point! And I didn't feel I was the one to be able to share any messages from the beyond from this powerhouse of a lady. I felt like I was still a complete beginner here!

But since Janet seemed adamant that she wasn't going anywhere, I timidly said, "It feels like I have Janet here." My eyes were still closed, but I could almost sense Pam rolling *her* eyes. Since Janet had passed recently, I was sure every one of her students thought they were connecting with her. I started describing other images coming through while Pam patiently guided me to continue saying what I was receiving, even though the things I was saying aloud seemed random and nothing specific that could identify Janet. Then, the image of an owl popped into my mind. It was not just any owl, but the same watercolor picture I had created the night before with various shades of blue all around.

*Great!* I thought. *Now, I'm mentally projecting my own artwork into the mix. Really?!*

Pam could sense that I was holding back and prodded me to just give what I was getting. I wasn't prepared to fully describe it yet, so I cautiously started with, "I see a bird."

Pam's ears perked up. "What kind of bird?"

I sighed, and then told her it was an owl and I heard the excitement in her voice as I continued to describe it. I knew this was somehow relevant, though I had no idea how. When I had finished my reading, Pam revealed to me that the owl was THE symbol that she associated with Janet and let her know that I did in fact connect with Janet today on her behalf! She had even given Janet a painting of an owl!

Astounded, and with truth chills running all over my body, I suddenly realized that the owl picture I'd created the night before was inspired by Janet, ahead of this meeting with Pam! It was all orchestrated by Spirit! Furthermore, I was beginning to understand how Spirit worked through me using my own experiences and imagery to convey messages. In Pam's words, "Sometimes it only takes that one key piece of evidence to let your sitter know it's their loved one."

Everyone always asks when you started practicing mediumship or psychic skills. Again, the real "practice" isn't the technical application or study, but the medium's emotional development that really begins, and deepens, the process.

> *"After all, how can you expect to correctly interpret and communicate the emotional state and heartfelt messages on behalf of the Spirit world if you are unable to even do this for yourself? Can you allow yourself to be vulnerable enough to lay bare the true essence of your own soul for the world to see? It takes this bravery, this courage, to do this, and it takes time to develop this aptitude and arrive at this place of willingness."*
>
> *~More nuggets of wisdom from Andy Byng*

At seventeen, I'd had my first spiritual awakening. I saw the entire world differently; I felt hope, purpose, and true connection for the first time in this lifetime. Though it seemed like I'd only been practicing mediumship and psychic development consciously and formally for the past couple of years, in actuality, I'd been doing the real work of learning to understand and manage my emotional and mental states for my entire adult life.

I'd always had belief and trust in all things metaphysical, including psychic and mediumship work, but never saw myself as having these abilities. In my teens and into my early twenties, I was interested in learning astrology, numerology, and palm reading, and I started doing readings for fun with my family. I also conducted tarot readings for myself, as well as making regular visits to local psychics. But, due to experiencing dark energies around me (especially at night in the hypnogogic state), I really wasn't keen on opening this up further. Fascinated by channeling and trance states, I'd read much of the Seth material and Edgar Cayce. I felt that I had a natural propensity for this type of channeling work, but I was closed off to the idea of surrendering to Spirit for fear that the wrong kind of energy would somehow take control of me. I know now that speaks to my negative emotional and mental state at that time.

In my thirties, my spiritual practice was placed on the backburner. After a six-year marriage ended in divorce, I went a little wild, partying and drinking – sometimes to the point of blacking out. To be completely honest, I was actually having fun during a good bit of the process, but I also knew this way of living – and of numbing my emotions – couldn't last.

The transition from age thirty-nine to forty was my next major awakening – a full-blown kundalini awakening, at that! I double-downed on my meditation practice and went deeper than ever with my spiritual practice. Though I'd experienced many incidents with spirit activity in the years before that, the profound mental, physical, emotional, and spiritual changes opened up new channels for receiving healing and guidance.

A significant memory and point of emotional "mastery" on my journey was my final surgery. At the time I didn't know if it would be my last one, but I was hopeful. I'd already had many surgeries and my previous team of doctors had run out of treatment options and hope. After being told that my only option was yet another surgery, which may or may not resolve this undiagnosed chronic issue but would definitely leave me having to wear a colostomy bag for the rest of my life, I knew it was time to find a new hospital and a new doctor.

Even after meeting with my new doctor, hope was hard to come by. He candidly told me that surgery was necessary and he didn't know what he'd uncover once he went inside, but he would do everything in his power and skill to resolve my issue once and for all. He said it was likely he'd have to do a total hysterectomy, though he may be able to keep one ovary. Would I be okay with this? I said that I trusted him to do whatever he felt was necessary, but if it was at all possible I'd prefer to keep one ovary so I'd have the choice if I ever decided I wanted to conceive.

Prior to the day of the surgery, I had consistently prayed for the infinite power of Source and any and all Divine support out there to please work through this doctor and the entire surgical team. Help them to help me. I then surrendered everything over to Spirit and put my faith in the hands of my medical team.

On the day of my surgery, I sat in a small medical room in my hospital gown feeling quite vulnerable and nervous, but also somehow calm, peaceful, and in good spirits despite the situation at hand. As one final act of self empowerment before having to go into full surrender mode, when it was time to be wheeled into the surgery room, I asked the nurses if I could bypass the use of the wheelchair and just walk myself into the surgery room, which was not the usual protocol. They said yes, and what followed was most surreal. I walked through the double doors of this sterile operating room, sat myself onto the operating table, laid back, looked up into the eyes of each person on my medical team gathered around me that day, and said, "Thank you so much for helping me. I have complete trust that you'll do your best." Shortly after that, I was out.

The surgery lasted seven hours. The doctor later said that there was so much buildup of some unknown fluid throughout my body that it had created "channels"; plus, there was a lot of scar tissue from all the other surgeries. Bottom line: it was very slow, very tedious, for him to work his way through. It required tremendous patience and skill, and in the end he was able to save one ovary. When he talked to my parents in the waiting room, he told them he couldn't believe how brave I was and how I handled everything with amazing grace and courage. I didn't tell him it was because I knew I had a team of the Divine working on my behalf!

I had definitely gained some scars from that whole experience, but I also knew that it left me with a whole new level of spiritual strength that can only come from having gone through a struggle of equal proportion.

My God, the drive to Crater Lake was absolutely amazing! There was a subtle mist over the water, creating a spectacular image that I wished I could take with my camera. There's no better art than that which is created in nature.

I think most artists would agree that the art they create didn't come from them, but rather was inspired by the muses of the Universe working through them. That has certainly been the case for me with my spirit portraits, as well as my photography.

It's no wonder that I was drawn to do wedding photography for many years, though my favorite was always street art. For both, you have to master the art of present awareness, tune in to everything happening around you and be ready for that spontaneous spark of inspiration in any given moment. You must be sensitive enough to first receive the inspiration, then follow that hunch immediately to capture that fleeting moment, be it the magical lighting, an expression, a gesture or – if you're "lucky" – a perfectly timed combination of all of these. And once the moment's gone, you can't get it back. It'll never be exactly the same.

There were times when I'd have this little nudge to take the shot, but hesitated or started to pass the opportunity. Then I'd get that gentle nudge again and follow the lead, only to happily discover later that it was one of the best pictures I'd ever taken.

## DAY SEVENTY-ONE

I woke early with a direct interpretation about my dream within a dream, which I quickly jotted down:

**No matter where you want to be,**
**this is where you are now.**
**EMBRACE IT.**

Later, in mediumship circle, Pam's words echoed the same message and even the same exact wording as she once again pointed out that we should all be working by now: *"It's time to move into embracing and working with your mediumship and integrating this into your everyday life!"*

Then, Pam led us through a meditation to activate our pineal gland, which is the psychic center for expanding consciousness. Almost as soon as she started, I fell into a deep state and began receiving a constant stream of downloads and messages of encouragement, including the following:

***When you embrace who you are,***
***others will too.***
**EMBRACE YOUR TRUE NATURE.**

The message continued:

***You've had many incarnations, but this is the lifetime that you will find balance between the physical and spiritual aspects.***

Then, I was shown an image of lines expanding into a larger triangle and heard the message:

**YOU CAN SEE BEYOND what others can see;**
**YOU CAN HEAR BEYOND what others can hear.**

I was then given a visual of the classic logic puzzle in which one is challenged to connect nine dots without lifting their pencil from the paper and using the fewest possible number of straight lines. The solution requires thinking and literally moving "outside the box." The message continued:

**The box represents self-imposed limitations that aren't real… it's an illusion, like the veil between the two worlds.**

**When you move past these limitations, you can stretch yourself further and all the dots will connect for you!**

CHAPTER ELEVEN

# DISRUPTION

***"There are times when the most difficult situations arise in your life. If you choose to, they can act as a catalyst to heal other areas… they're truly your greatest teachers.***

**~ John Holland**
**The Psychic Tarot Oracle Deck**

# DAY SEVENTY-TWO

## Klamath Falls to Bend, OR

It's always much appreciated when I have an easy transition day, and today was one of those. I was also thrilled to find that the place I rented was actually between Bend and Sisters, tucked away in the Ponderosa Pines. I was looking forward to exploring the area.

Being continuously between spaces, I'd become mindful of how this manifests in various physical, mental, emotional ways and I felt thankful for the transformation that was happening. It was necessary and I welcomed it today, embracing the uncomfortable.

As I sipped my coffee, I heard "Long Blue Line" by Leif Vollebeck playing in my mind. I had been listening to the song a lot on my hikes, ever since it showed up as a suggestion on Spotify a couple of weeks earlier. The lyrics, about uncertainty over one's direction, spoke to how I'd been feeling. As the author of one article put it, Vollebeck's song "captured the solitude that arises in between the coming and the going..." Perfectly said!

Lately, I'd felt stuck on where to go next. I was drawn to go back East for a visit, and spend time this summer in Lilydale, New York, but the details of how to get there and where to stay in the meantime eluded me. No matter where I decided to go next, I knew this whole trip had already changed me significantly and I trusted that would continue.

When I rolled into Bend, I saw a Barnes & Noble and decided to check out their selection of tarot cards and books. While I was exploring their metaphysical shelves, two young girls who appeared to be no older than twenty strolled up. One of the girls was giving book recommendations to her friend. I overheard her talking about how she planned to be a life coach, because she wouldn't have to actually go in depth into any one particular subject in terms of study or learning and could make good money giving advice to people in a variety of general areas. Wow! I wasn't sure whether to laugh or gasp aloud, but was able to politely stifle both. I chalked her naive comments up to her age, but how unfortunate to have that a mind-set…thinking she could be a "life coach" without having any life experience or needing to reach any depth of knowledge or spiritual growth!

It's like people trying to reach "enlightenment" through the shortcut of ayahuasca or other mind-altering drugs. Yes, they can help get your mind out of the way and give you a brief glimpse beyond this limited reality, but they are short-lived, take you deep quicker than most are prepared for, and can be accompanied by some nasty side effects. Sorry, but there is no shortcut to self-awareness. It requires time, patience, willingness, dedicated practice, and commitment. There's just no way around it.

> ***"...there are no shortcuts to knowledge, to wisdom, to understanding- these must be lived, must be experienced by each and every soul."***
>
> **~Edgar Cayce reading 830-2**

The drive to my new rental space was so smooth, and as soon as I started the last stretch I had a sense that it felt right. Driving up the gravel road, through this forest area of pines with the Cascades as the backdrop, I came upon the home which looked just like in the pictures. I was greeted downstairs by one of the hosts, then I went upstairs. As soon as I saw the space, I felt peaceful, comfortable. I felt more at home than I had in some time.

I had a beautiful, spacious apartment all to myself on a gorgeous, wooded lot. There was a private deck, surrounded by trees and the sounds of nature. Gratitude filled me for the guidance to reserve this space, and that I had followed it.

# DAY SEVENTY-FOUR

I felt like a new person after a restful night's sleep and had a nice one-on-one mentoring session with Pam. I so appreciated her experience, wisdom, compassion, and perspective. It was like talking with a friend who just happened to be super-wise and intuitive!

She reminded me of my reading for her the day before and said it was fascinating to watch the quick shift I made in response to her feedback – at first, she'd observed that I was starting to question things and get in my own way. Immediately following that, I had taken a deep breath and got out of my head to go deeper with Spirit and back into the flow of the true message, which ended up being very accurate. It served as a wonderful learning opportunity for me. I knew the Universe was conspiring and arranging opportunities for my growth.

After Pam and I said our goodbyes, I jumped over to my other work with my speech pathology students. I was so proud of them, seeing how they had matured and blossomed across the school year, and I was moved to hear some say how they would miss me over the summer. I felt so blessed to work with them. They helped me as much as I helped them, uplifting my spirit and energy whenever we worked together.

With my sessions done, I decided to explore a nearby trail. It was already afternoon, and I figured I'd go for a few miles and simply turn around when I was tired. Instead, over ten miles of hiking and trail running later, I arrived back at my car, my poor feet definitely feeling the last few miles, but in a satisfying way. My body, mind, and soul were obviously craving this extra time in nature. I felt strong and rejuvenated.

In my pre-dinner meditation, I immediately felt myself plug in with a strong vibrating energy that pulsed throughout my whole body. I could literally feel my body shaking, as if someone was moving the couch under me (at one point I even took a quick peek to check!). I welcomed and was excited by this sensation, for there is nothing better than knowing without a doubt that I am connected to Spirit. I am so appreciative for the sensitivity and awareness to perceive and experience this for myself, and on behalf of people who are not able to do so for themselves.

With dinner, I watched the emotional final episode of a show I'd been enjoying called *Nine Perfect Strangers.* It so clearly portrayed the intense grief and desire to reconnect with loved ones who'd crossed over, and reminded me how sacred this work is that I'm doing. We must always be mindful of the vulnerable place many of our clients are in, which is why they are coming to us.

## DAY SEVENTY-FIVE

My dreams last night were unpleasant, touching on past memories and taking me back to real life scenes in which I had set clear boundaries and firmly communicated to others what they didn't want to hear, but needed to.

When I woke to this, I called to my unseen helpers to please help clear these memories from my cells; I also thanked them for the awareness that these memories were still present and now ready to be released. I visualized these and any other old thoughts and feelings that no longer served me being flushed from my body. Cutting cords that were very faint now, but apparently still present... letting go... releasing... clearing.

Every obstacle, every unsettling feeling and uncomfortable situation I have encountered, forces me to focus more clearly than ever and reconnect in a powerful way to my true self and my Divine team in order bring about the changes I want to see, feel, and experience. As I raise my own vibration and become more of who I am in living my soul's purpose, I transform not only myself but the world around me.

In my first therapy session this morning, my client – a graduating senior with high-functioning autism with whom I'd worked for years – began to appear very anxious and stressed. He complained of his chronic pain. I had to walk him through the mindful breathing and calming strategies we had been working on together all year.

Once calm, he shared some observations about his life and how the many ongoing difficulties he had faced related to his diagnoses of autism, anxiety, and other medical issues had forced him learn perseverance. I listened in awe at this young man's self-awareness, wisdom, and insight. Of course, I couldn't fail to notice that it was perfectly in sync with the same insight I'd received just that morning. Truly, there are no coincidences!

When it was time to wrap up our final session, he was so sweet, thanking me for my teachings over the years and saying how lucky he'd been to know me and work with me. His words expressed exactly what I was feeling, that it had been such a gift to work with him. I was truly the lucky one here, and I couldn't have been prouder!

Yesterday, I had been messaging with the Airbnb host to see if I could extend my stay. She already had it reserved for the weekend but suggested I go somewhere for a couple of days and return next week. However, the more I tried to make the details come together, the more it felt like things weren't making sense. That's what happens when you try to make things happen or force things versus allowing inspiration to flow to you on its own.

After letting it marinate overnight, a new idea came to me regarding my next destination: Salt Lake City! It felt like the perfect transition place or jumping-off point for wherever I was called to next. I also kept feeling drawn back East, specifically Lilydale. Just that morning I was guided to a movie about Lilydale that I'd never heard of but looked forward to watching soon.

I had planned to head into Bend that afternoon to pick up a few items; however, when I got to the main road to turn right, I found myself pulled toward the opposite direction. Of course, I followed my intuition and ended up in the small nearby town of Sisters.

While driving there, the thought dropped in that:

**Sometimes when things make the least sense, you can trust more than ever that it's probably your intuition guiding you.**

I grabbed a hot latte, then stopped at a gift shop and apothecary. Sharrie, the shop's owner, was so nice and had created a lovely space with a bevy of beauty and wellbeing products. What got my attention, however, is when she shared that the store was result of her midlife shift. She added, ***"It's so worth the risk to take that leap of faith and do what you know to be right for yourself."*** Another perfectly orchestrated connection offering me a message of encouragement!

## DAY SEVENTY-SIX

I felt odd all day, as if I was running out of time and still unclear on what I was really supposed to do to with everything I'd gathered along this journey so far. I had been given inspiration on several creative projects, but I knew some of those would come later on down the line.

I also felt like this nomadic lifestyle may be drawing to a close soon, but I hadn't yet discovered a place to land. This led to a deeper contemplation of the time I had left on Earth and how I wanted to make sure I accomplish whatever it is I had preplanned for myself in this incarnation. It reminded me of the Wayne Dyer quote:

***"Don't die with your music still in you."***

For me, this translated to:

**Don't allow yourself to live any life other than the one you were born to live.**

When I pulled a tarot card for some inspiration, I received the Disruption card, which is The Tower in traditional tarot. While this may appear to be a negative sign to most people, actually it symbolizes a time of major transformation and even the step before enlightenment, if you allow it.

> ***"There are times when the most difficult situations arise in your life. If you choose to, they can act as a catalyst to heal other areas. They're beneficial because they're truly your greatest teachers. Learn from past mistakes, accept them, and integrate them into your life as stepping stones."***
>
> **~ The Psychic Tarot Oracle Deck by John Holland**

Yes, this was a dramatic time of major changes in my life, but I was thankful for the transformation of my body, mind, and soul. "Thank you for this opportunity for growth," I said. I was going to keep setting the intention to learn from challenges and saying this affirmation moving forward.

Then, having had enough seriousness for one night, I gave myself permission to take a well-deserved break, shake things off, and lighten it up with the help of a glass of red wine and a new show on Apple TV, *High Desert.* It was based on one of my new favorite places and one to which I hoped to return – Joshua Tree. Plus, the show looked hilarious.

## DAY SEVENTY-SEVEN

Dream Tarot: I woke to the image of a tarot card that was given to me in my dream. In the image, I was shown a figure of glowing white light, which represented me. The title on the card in large letters said:

**RENEWAL – SOUL GROWTH**

I was sure to start my day with my usual meditation. Yesterday, I had done something very uncharacteristic – jumping right into emails and planning for work – and ended up feeling irritable. It was a great reminder of the huge difference meditating first thing makes in the trajectory of my day.

I also tried to start each day with something inspirational or uplifting and lighthearted. I've seen that whatever energy I cultivate in the morning carries out for the rest of my day so I might as well choose the path to be a positive one.

Today, I had another uplifting activity to do as well. It was my dad's birthday, and my parents were on vacation to celebrate it. My heart smiled as I made arrangements for a surprise lobster dinner as his gift. Certainly, if anyone deserved a nice vacation and retirement, it was my parents. Talk about living through difficult life situations! They'd had more than their fair share and yet they were always so generous to everyone else. It was high time they enjoyed the fruits of all their labor and receive reciprocity for the kindness they put out into the world.

I then watched a Caroline Cory video in which she talked about the disconnection between our heads and hearts and how so many people focus on what's logical and expected, instead of what their own soul needs.

> ***"People have a huge misunderstanding that when you focus on self-preservation and self-love, you're kind of isolating yourself and it's the exact opposite."***
>
> **~Caroline Cory**

This was exactly what I'd been feeling – like I had been "isolating" myself but aware that it was necessary during this time in my life. Though carving out this time and space to focus on self-development did, to a large extent, keep me isolated, it was also freeing me from the distractions that often come in the form of expectations and needs of others, which had taken over my life for the past decade. This sense of urgency, that I was running out of time, was largely due to the fact that I had delayed this move for so long, despite my knowing deep down that it would eventually come calling.

When you focus on self-love, you are actually doing so much more good for the people and world around you than you ever could by being in the middle of their problems trying to "help" them. When we raise our vibration and consciousness, it powerfully influences those around us. Even if I never did another reading, produced another course or created another piece of art, but continued to focus on raising my vibration, I'd still be contributing to positive change in the world.

On this new day, I was turning a corner and once again felt uplifted and inspired. This transformation had definitely been a process – indeed, one that often felt like a "Disruption" – but that was part of letting go of those old patterns and other crap I'd been lugging around. When these things came up for release, all I had to do was allow and shed the old skin so I could step into the newer, more empowered version of myself. A disruption of the old life in order to allow in the new.

I appreciated this time I was spending on my own, though I so looked forward to connecting with more like-minded souls, both in friendship and a romantic relationship with my soulmate. I appreciated this time of exploring, but I also looked forward to one day having a place to call home. I trusted that I'd get there eventually; for now, I was taking the long, scenic route, destination TBD!

My mantra for today:

**I LOVE WHO I AM**
**I LOVE WHO I AM BECOMING**
**I APPRECIATE WHERE I AM**
**I LOOK FORWARD TO WHERE I'M GOING**

# DAY SEVENTY-EIGHT

## Sisters, OR to Boise, ID

*"The power is the ocean and you are a fish in it.*
*We just have the illusion of separateness.*
*Let go of the illusion.*
*YOU ARE ALWAYS IN THE POWER.*
*We are always one with the power of Spirit.*
*All of us are connected... always."*

**~Pam Meredith**

I woke at 5:30 with a busy morning ahead of me: my seven o'clock mediumship circle, followed by check-out at ten and my drive to Boise.

When I arrived (via Zoom) for our circle, we were placed in small group break-out rooms to perform platform mediumship. I was so blessed to be placed with three other women I admire and whose energy I just love.

I set the intention for the Spirit world to please bring forth someone closely related to my sitter and to offer a message that was most helpful and healing to whomever needed it most.

Before we even started, I could see and sense a young man I felt might be related to Jodi, one of the women in the group. Of course, in these exercises, each medium – and the spirit person they are communicating with – must wait their turn. The young man tried coming through right away, but then politely hung back in my "waiting room." At some point, though, my heartbeat was pumping faster and faster and I knew I needed to dive in and give him the podium.

It was such a beautiful and emotional reading. As I had initially sensed, this was Jodi's son, who it seemed had passed in his twenties. He had shown me her face right away, confirming this and let me know he was coming through to communicate clear evidence so that his mom would know that, without a doubt, it was him. Once this was established, he was able to deliver his loving messages for her.

He was so revved up and full of life and I could feel chills and energy moving all the way through my fingertips! He was an old soul... wise. He shared that he'd had an awareness that he was not long for this world; that's why he made sure he lived life to the fullest and did not waste a single day. He had lived more in his short time on Earth than most people who live to be ninety.

As his soul blended further with mine, he made me aware of his overwhelming love for his mother. He also wanted her to know that though he didn't always come forward during readings, he was always with her.

***"We're always connected,"*** he emphasized.

After his message was complete, Jodi confirmed almost all of the information, including the fact that her son, whose name was Anthony, doesn't always come through. What an honor that he had placed his trust in me and knew I would be able to communicate his true essence! The whole group was touched, but none more so than me and Jodi.

Ask any medium and they will tell you that feeling into the age of a communicator can be tricky; for example, a spirit person who lived to be eighty can present at a much younger age, perhaps to indicate that time in their human life or express how young and healthy they are on the other side. It turned out that Anthony had passed at only sixteen years of age; however, Jodi shared that mediums often interpreted him to pass in his twenties because he was so emotionally and spiritually mature for his age. He was truly an old soul! She added that even the paramedics on the scene of his accident had thought he was twenty-one or twenty-two years old.

Anthony was such a bright beautiful light who had touched the lives of so many people. Jodi lovingly shared that he would "make time for anyone who needed a friend and he hated seeing people suffer." At his funeral, crowds of people had flocked in to say their goodbyes and honor his life. That's how big of an impact he had made.

Even as I wrote this in my journal, I felt truth chills all over my body and knew that Anthony's powerful angelic spirit would continue to watch over his mom – and perhaps me too, because we were now connected at a soul level.

"Angel Photo" credited to Anthony

**"Don't waste a single day."**

~Anthony J. Higginbottom

Later, while on the road, I kept thinking about the reading and how honored I was that Jodi's son had trusted me enough to interpret his messages to his mom – and so thankful that I hadn't let either of them down. I had given many accurate readings before, but for some reason this experience had cracked my heart completely open. *My God,* I thought, just letting the tears flow, *I am so grateful for the sacredness of this work, and I never want to take that for granted.*

On the way out, I saw that I had about half a tank of gas. I probably needed more than that to make it to Boise, over five hours away, but I figured I'd stop at a rest stop along the highway for a fill-up and a bathroom break. Then, while waiting at a light at the last turn out of town, I got the feeling like, "This is your last chance to gas up before hitting the road." Nah, I told myself, there would be plenty of stations on the way... only there wasn't. I was on a long, lonely road in the Oregon Badlands, which was beautiful but without towns, without people, and – most importantly – without gas stations.

The further I drove, the more I wondered if I needed to look at a turn-off to a different road. I called out to my spirit team and asked them to please help me out with a gas station and a bathroom – soon! Not ten minutes later, I saw a cafe/gas station! It was expensive, five dollars a gallon, but I was happy to pay and not have to worry about this anymore. And, they had a clean bathroom inside. Thank you, team!

**Note to Self:**

**Next time, follow the subtle nudge when you're sitting at the light...**

**It'll always steer you in the right direction And it'll save you both money and needless worry.**

# DAY SEVENTY-NINE

## Salt Lake City, UT

As I turned off the exit toward downtown SLC, I saw a man on the side of the road with a sign asking for donations. I gave him twenty dollars and told him I hoped it would be helpful to him today.

He was so appreciative and said, "There should be more people in the world like you."

"And there should be more people in the world like you, too," I replied.

We've all needed help at some point in our lives, and we all need to do our part to help others. I prayed that he be surrounded by support and protection and that he would find himself in a stable position one day soon.

After arriving at my Airbnb, I unpacked and then sat down for a meditation to ground myself to this place, clear the space, and embed it with renewed energy. I kept hearing the message that: ***"when I heal myself, I heal others too."***

Even as I worked energetically, I was aware that I was not loving my new "home," which was not exactly as depicted in the listing. However, since I was already settled and there were no refunds, I decided to see this as another opportunity to embrace the uncomfortable, honor the time and space between, and, with gratitude, utilize it to be creative and allow further healing and rest.

CHAPTER TWELVE

# MESSAGES FROM SPIRIT

***"Mediumship is not just about the evidential communication; it also provides a valuable time for healing. As a medium, you're blessed to have the opportunity to become the conduit of these beautiful and empowering messages."***

**~ John Holland and Lauren Rainbow from the Mediumship Training Deck**

# DAY EIGHTY

## Salt Lake City, UT

I woke remembering some interesting dreams, including one about Jared in which he said he loved and missed me while I held his hand to comfort him. I hated the thought of hurting him, and even though I knew it was the right decision to leave I was processing my own sadness as well. I had truly loved him and tried so hard to make our relationship work over the years. Now, I wanted only happiness for him and for his family.

As I went about my morning, I was still trying to adjust to this new place, which definitely was not my favorite. Then, remembering the sweet man living on the streets I'd met yesterday, I expressed appreciation for having a roof over my head when so many don't.

I eagerly signed into my regular psychic development circle, with the community I adored connecting with each week and the much-needed continuity wherever I found myself. It gave me a sense of purpose and belonging. During our guided group meditation, I was shown the **HOPE** tarot card in my mind's eye with the following message:

***You are surrounded by light.***
***You have such a bright light in your heart and***
***you will share this with the world through your work.***

# DAY EIGHTY-ONE

As I ate breakfast, I savored both the food and an interview with Irish author Lorna Byrne, who writes about her experiences with the angelic realm. Indeed, her energy felt angelic, and it was comforting to hear someone else so casually and frankly describe their everyday interactions with angels and spirits, which would seem unbelievable to most people. Just as she was talking about the signs, including feathers, that we get from angels, I walked into the bathroom and noticed the tiniest little white feather on the floor! I was then guided to look at Lorna's website and saw she was not only going to be at the Omega Institute in New York but Boone, North Carolina. Smiling, I put these in the mental file as possibilities. Whether or not I ended up attending either event, it was definitely another angelic sign pulling me back East to both NC and NY in the near future.

Last night before bed, I'd sent a message to the host of a rental not far from Yellowstone National Park, which I was wanting to visit. This morning, I received a response with a special invitation to book. My next destination was secured! Afterward, I'd continue my journey eastward but would wait to figure out the details. For now, I was calm knowing the next step.

In the early afternoon, I had two on-point readings during a Spirit Art class through Arthur Findlay. One reading was actually for the instructor and the other was for someone I'd not met before. Both were ninety-five to one hundred percent accurate in the evidence, which was shown through imagery and symbols, and it felt wonderful to so clearly deliver messages on behalf of the Spirit world for these two ladies.

After class, I sat for a few hours at a local coffeeshop to work on billing and paperwork. Having to balance my "day job" with everything else was challenging at times, and there was still more to finish tomorrow. At least I was in the homestretch before summer break.

It struck me how strangely time moved on this journey, toggling between very slow and very rapid – and all simultaneously! The last few months had felt more like years, and I felt like a very different person living a very different life. It felt strange, but good.

## DAY EIGHTY-TWO

I woke this morning at 5:30, even though I didn't have to get up until 6:30. While the extra hour of sleep would have been nice, I barely noticed; my body was simply set on that earlier internal time clock. I was instead consumed with a dream that had left me feeling completely devastated. In the dream:

*I had just ended a long-term relationship and was chastising my partner for how badly he had treated me (which was the reason for the breakup.) Afterward, I was in a room with stacks of my old journals, crying and grieving deeply over the loss. In the journals, I was telling a friend how I had saved all his love letters to me since the first day we met. I said that I had tried so hard for years to make things work. I was feeling such deep sorrow, at a soul level, for the loss.*

I woke still feeling this intense sadness, but not sure why it was coming up for me now. I'd thought I was over it.

My relationship with Jared had so many flaws from day one and had been a very rocky road. I had tolerated so much mistreatment across the years until I was finally fed up with it and started stepping into my power. I was at least able to speak my truth and set boundaries near the end, but it wasn't well-received, to say the least, and seemed to create more problems than solutions. I think we both always knew that the relationship wasn't meant to last. I won't say I stayed too long, because timing is relative to when you feel ready to finally make a change. And, for a long time I had an inner urge telling me there was still more to mine from the relationship, still something to learn, and that I needed to resolve some recurring patterns or karma in my life before moving on, lest I take these lessons with me into the next relationship. The problem was that instead of mining for gems, we just seemed to be digging ourselves deeper into a hole that we could never seem to get out of.

Why, given my confidence that my decision to leave was the right one, did I feel such sorrow in my dream last night? Endings can be bittersweet, I thought, and then the truth hit me. I had always planned to devote my life to Jared and hadn't yet allowed my heart to grieve properly. My dream had revealed emotions I was not aware of in my conscious waking state but still needed to be cleared from the heart space.

**We need to become aware of our blocks and the stories behind them and face the uncomfortable feelings – not to feed them, but to FEEL them in order to release them. It's when we try to suppress or block uncomfortable feelings that we create struggle and keep them stuck. Instead, if we let go of the resistance and allow them to come up, we can move on.**

This was essentially a ***dream healing!*** My soul was forcing me, through my dreams, to see what I'd been suppressing. This allowed me to witness my own story and feel the deep pain and grief while in a safe space. Also, I knew it was healing me in ways that went far beyond this relationship. *Thank you for showing me what needs to be released.*

After finishing work, I felt tired, emotionally spent. I picked up a coffee and a snack and headed to the Great Salt Lake. I needed to be away from the apartment, away from this computer, and to be surrounded by the healing and the grounding touch of Mother nature.

As I headed onto the highway, I was so lost in my thoughts that I ended up going the wrong way. After quickly rerouting my directions, I was instructed to take the next exit and make a U-Turn to head back in the opposite direction. I made the turn, then pulled to a stop at a red light. While waiting for it to change, I saw a man standing on the side of the road with his dog, asking for assistance.

Without hesitation, my hand reached down and pulled a twenty from my wallet to give to him before the light could change. He was so pleasantly surprised and flashed me the biggest, sweetest smile. I told him he had a beautiful dog and that I hoped this would help them a little today. He exclaimed, "This will help a lot! I was so worried and didn't know what we were going to do today. Now I can get him a bag of dog food and something for me to eat too. Thank you!" I told him how happy I was that I came this way and I was so lucky to have the chance to meet him. Driving back onto the highway, I smiled, knowing that I hadn't taken a wrong turn at all; I was guided to go this way. It was all divinely orchestrated. I am always so thankful to be a messenger and helper whenever and wherever I can. I felt so honored to be able to give him just a little bit of happiness, comfort, and hope today, and I had no doubt that our teams of guardian angels had collaborated to make this happen.

If I did nothing else while in SLC besides meeting and delivering assistance, a kind word, and a smile to the two men I had met, I had fulfilled my purpose there. It makes me think of the young man busking for money on a street in Fayetteville, North Carolina whom I'd met a few days before heading out on this Soul Trip. I recalled feeling as though I had seen a reflection of God in that young man's face, and I felt that again now. Maybe they were angels who'd taken human form to uplift me and give me the opportunity to feel helpful and purposeful. Maybe I was simply witnessing another's experience. Either way, I was glad to be part of the plan.

Once I arrived at Great Salt Lake Park, I walked down the path to some benches by the water where I'd have some privacy. It started to rain a bit, but I didn't care. I just sat there, letting the water sprinkle over me. It felt refreshing. After a bit, I walked, still sipping my coffee, to the other side of the beach area. There weren't many people there this time of the day, save a couple stacking prayer rocks and a few others. I took pictures of the numerous towers amidst the lake, mountains and storm clouds framed behind them. The scene was a photographer's dream, and I had a ball snapping up pictures from every angle. Then I sat down in the center of all the prayer rocks in this sacred space, closed my eyes, and just listened to the sound of the waves. It was exactly what my soul needed, and certainly worth more than the five-dollar entry fee!

## DAY EIGHTY-THREE

While getting myself ready for my day, I was listening to the audiobook of Lorna Byrne's *Angels in my Hair.* I loved hearing about her experience with angels and thinking about my communication and experiences with them as well. I looked forward to continuing to strengthen and deepen my relationship with them, along with the healers, helpers, guides, and guardian angels that surround me.

Inspired to pull one card from my Mediumship Training Deck, I teared up when I saw the message I'd been asking for. The card, titled Messages from Spirit, depicted a colorful butterfly with the words "You are loved" flowing forth. The back of the card read:

***"Mediumship is not just about the evidential communication;<br>it also provides a valuable time for healing.***

***As a medium, you're blessed to have the opportunity to become<br>the conduit of these beautiful and empowering messages.***

***Our spirit loved ones work hard to connect with us to facilitate<br>these heart-centered communications, so being open<br>to receive is a vitally important mindset to have."***

Today felt like a good day to visit Antelope Island State Park, one of a couple of places on my Salt Lake City bucket list. The park was about an hour away and I really enjoyed the drive, relaxing and listening to my tunes along the way. I had read a little about the park and the wildlife there, but it was even more expansive and beautiful than I had imagined. The scenery was just gorgeous! I was just fine being the slow, "old lady driver" today, letting others fly by while I savored a lazy scenic route all over the island, stopping many times to walk and snap tons of pictures.

My favorite experience was being up close to the herds of bison that freely roamed the island and watching them graze and move about. I hadn't anticipated spending so much time there, but before I knew it hours had flown by. It felt so good being out in nature and exploring a setting unlike any I'd seen before.

## DAY EIGHTY-FOUR

I woke to my alarm at 5 a.m., very excited for my trip to the Bonneville Salt Flats, which I'd read about and seen pictures of online. Dressing quickly, I was out the door by 5:30 so I could arrive as close to sunrise as possible.

On the way out of town I stopped at a McDonald's to grab a hot coffee for the hour-and-a-half ride there. There was a man sitting down near the drive-thru lanes; he approached me and politely asked if I wouldn't mind buying him a breakfast sandwich. I was happy to do so and ended up getting him two full meals with coffees. He looked at me wide-eyed and smiling and asked, "Why are you so nice?" We chatted while we waited on the order. I learned his name was Sean, and he had a girlfriend nearby who was hungry as well, so I was glad I followed the inspiration to order more food! Before parting ways, we shook hands and I wished him a wonderful rest of his day. It felt so good to see him happily and proudly walking back to where his girlfriend was waiting so he could deliver her the surprise of a nice hot breakfast.

I enjoyed an easy drive, sipping hot coffee, listening to music, and enjoying the gorgeous scenery. The windows were down with crisp air flowing in. When I arrived there were a few other people there for pictures, but it wasn't crowded, which I'd figured would be the case this early. Otherworldly and magical, the landscape was perfect for photo inspiration. I captured so many awesome shots. It was well worth getting up at 5 a.m. for this!

After returning to SLC, I ran out for a nice hike to get some physical movement and fresh air, and simply plant my feet on the ground. I took a new trail that overlooked the city and along the way received many beautiful signs of love and support. I saw a rock shaped like a heart and couldn't pass up the opportunity to take it home with me. Then I saw a huge white feather, which reminded me of Lorna Byne and her mention of angels leaving feathers as signs. And, finally, I passed by the biggest daffodil I'd ever seen in my life and was sure to make a wish.

I only had one more day here and then I'd leave for Idaho. I'd enjoyed all the surrounding areas and had some really great unexpected experiences, but I was looking forward to moving on; first stop: another intriguing location called Craters of the Moon, which I was excited to visit. After that, I'd have a short stay at a rental not too far from Yellowstone before most likely winding my way back home to visit my parents for my birthday and Father's Day.

CHAPTER THIRTEEN

# TRUTH

***"Spiritual awakening, clarity, the revelation of truth, and cosmic consciousness. What was once not obvious will now be realized and understood."***

**~John Holland from**
**The Psychic Tarot**

# DAY EIGHTY-SIX

## SLC to Craters of the Moon and Rexburg, ID

Waking just before my alarm, I quickly jotted down some dreams before getting ready to head out.

**DREAM #1:** It's nighttime and I'm outside climbing fences looking for "alien" visitors. I am talking with a friend, saying how no one would believe it if I told them where I'm really from.

**DREAM #2:** Felt more like a visitation than a dream. I see a blue light from which two beings emerge. One is blue with large dark eyes and the other looks human-like with longer blond hair. They tell me I'd previously incarnated as different beings on different worlds and that the reason I've never felt like I've belonged anywhere is that I'm not really from here.

**DREAM #3:** I hear a woman commenting with relief that she can finally feel like she's done enough. Then, she's being asked by her spirit team, "What is enough? You'll never really be done."

After typing up my dreams, I pulled a salad from the fridge – an unorthodox breakfast, for sure, but I didn't want to waste it. As I ate, I watched a Caroline Cory video with a title that made me laugh: *Are You an Alien?* Appropriate, considering my dreams last night and the other experiences I'd had over the last few months relating to the whole starseed concept. I certainly felt like an alien a lot of the time! I recalled again the reading Michael had given me before I embarked on this journey. "You're not from here..." he'd commented, "...although I don't know where the hell you *are* from." At the time, I was thinking more along the lines of Panama,

Berlin, or Korea – not another planet! And the irony that I would soon be headed to The Craters of the Moon was certainly not lost on me. Seriously, you cannot make this stuff up!

After an easy drive from SLC, I spent a few hours exploring the Craters of the Moon National Monument & Preserve. I was struck by the otherworldliness of this place, with its expansive sea of grey, remnants of ancient lava flows, spanning as far as the eye could see. I really felt as though I had landed on the moon! As I walked along the trails, the individual rocks sparkled with various peacock shades of blue and purple under the blazing hot sun. Apparently, back in '69, Apollo 14 astronauts had actually trained here to prepare for their moon missions. This brought to mind the great Dr. Edgar Mitchell, the sixth man to walk on the moon. Mitchell's profound experience of oneness, or *samadhi*, as he looked upon Earth from space had led to a lifelong exploration of consciousness and the founding of the Institute of Noetic Sciences, still in existence today. Now, as I explored this picturesque and lonely space, and imagined what it must have been like to experience an actual moon landing, I felt as though I was walking in his footsteps.

Suddenly, a guy appeared, seemingly out of nowhere, and asked me to take some pictures of him. He saw my infinity tattoo on my wrist and asked me about the meaning, which led into a really nice conversation. I could tell he wanted to keep talking and get to know me better, but I politely wished him well and kept moving on. I wanted to continue exploring the park and still make good time for the rest of my drive to Rexburg, where I'd be staying.

On the way out, I stopped at the visitor's center to use the restroom. Then, as I was preparing to back out of the parking space to return to the highway, guess who pulled up right next to me? The same guy! Laughing at the synchronicity, I rolled down my window to say hi and again we chatted for a bit. After a while I noticed that I had a car waiting behind me. I guessed that this was probably an "arranged" meeting and I could have pulled over to chat more, but I just didn't want to go down that road today and give him any romantic notions. I appreciated that per my requests to the Universe, the possibility of love was now coming into my manifested experience, but neither this person nor the timing felt right in that moment. So I quickly said my goodbyes for the second time, though the disappointment on his face wasn't lost on me.

On the drive home, I'd thought about the phrase I'd read at the visitor's center to describe the Craters of the Moon: ***"A violent past, calm present, and uncertain future."*** It was said that the volcanoes there were dormant – not dead, just sleeping. Then, after arriving at my new "home" for the next few days, I was greeted by a picture hanging on the wall that read, ***"And just when the caterpillar thought the world was over, it became a butterfly."***

Both of these quotes seemed to perfectly reflect my own transformation.

## DAY EIGHTY-SEVEN

### Rexburg, ID

I drove out to, Jackson hole, Teton Village, and the Teton National Park. It was nothing short of breathtaking, but I was feeling under the weather and tired. I didn't take even one picture, and after a relatively short visit I was guided to head "home," do a healing meditation, and call it a day. I'd been on the go so much and today I just needed to get some rest.

There was some construction on the road, and one of the workers, who was directing traffic, was smiling, dancing around, and waving at people. Talk about enjoying your work! If everyone put that much enthusiasm and love into their job they'd be so much happier! I smiled and waved back at him, his energy uplifting me and everyone around him.

When I got back, I had a little snack and checked emails before my healing meditation. I was pleased to see an email from a woman I'd met about a year ago when I'd recorded a YouTube video for her on how to incorporate mindfulness and breathing techniques, whether into therapy practices or our daily lives. She was inviting me as a guest teacher for her online workshop on cultivating presence and was very complimentary about my work, which was so appreciated.

I'd also received a nice email from one of my mentors, who again encouraged me to offer my psychic and mediumship services; I just had to have the courage to do it, she said. I had actually already started doing this over the past few weeks, but her note motivated me to do so on a more regular basis.

That evening, I looked at the clock and noted that it was 10:10 – an angel number signifying manifestation, alignment, endings, and new beginnings. I was grateful for the message, and so tired that at that moment my focus was on manifesting a good night's sleep! I planned to get up early and visit Yellowstone, the whole reason I came to this area in the first place. And I definitely planned to take pictures this time.

## DAY EIGHTY-EIGHT

Before driving to Yellowstone, I participated in an Auragraphs workshop through Arthur Findlay. Auragraphs are a wonderful way to depict symbols, inspired by and fed to us by the Spirit world, as evidence of a crossed-over loved one, as well as messages that will be helpful to the person receiving the reading. The workshop was fascinating, and I had a wonderful session giving and receiving readings with Brent, who was in Charlotte, North Carolina! Such a small world!

I brought forth one of Brent's ancestors and one related to his wife, both who gave me solid evidence that was easily recognized and highly relevant to his life. Brent connected with someone I did not recognize, but I loved the helpful messaging, which was the same as the one I recently received when I drew the magical genie card for myself. The message had even cropped up in a meditation, when I'd been told to determine what I wanted to see for myself and focus my energy there. I had been advised, "You have everything at your fingertips, you can go in any direction and you'll be successful. You have many options, but now you get to choose." So when Brent described a genie lamp and a granting of wishes, I knew he was accurately receiving information.

Before leaving for Yellowstone, I noted the forecast calling for thunderstorms and wondered if I should go. I decided to chance it and went on to enjoy completely clear beautiful blue skies! A great reminder to trust that all will work out.

As I made my way through the Teton National Forest and just before reaching the south entry station to Yellowstone, I could see mass areas of trees that were burned in the many forest fires that had ravaged this area. I noticed how bright it seemed here due to all of the leafy coverage having been cleared. It made me think of the analogy of how something destructive in our lives can shed new light on a situation and give us a clearer view than before. It also allows rebirth to happen. As I entered another part of the forest, getting closer to Yellowstone, I could see new trees springing forth. Like the symbolism of a phoenix! First the burning of the fire, and then the rebirth.

## DAY EIGHTY-NINE

Already the final full day was here, and with no decision as to my next destination, I was really cutting it close to the wire!

This morning, I recalled three pretty amazing "dreams" that were so visceral, so real, I wondered whether they were actually some sort of ethereal travel!

**DREAM 1:** A young woman appeared and repeatedly told me that I need to ***accept help from people around me.***

**DREAM 2:** I felt the powerful presence of Archangel Michael. He showed up like I'd seen in pictures – strong, with blonde flowing hair, huge wings, and a golden glow. Michael said he was here to give me strength, remind me of my inner power, and offer healing and comfort. He said that I'm very strong, but I need to allow some healing and assistance. He also said that I'm infinitely supported by the angels and I have the heart of an angel. Then he wrapped his angel wings around me and hugged me and I was surrounded by his golden light. I started to cry and he put his hand on my heart and said that the crying was a good sign; it meant I was allowing the healing into my heart.

**DREAM 3**: I saw and felt myself being lifted up out of my body. At first I was holding a golden balloon, but then I heard a voice tell me I don't need the balloon... I can fly without it. Releasing the balloon, I floated upward towards a huge ball of light. I then felt energy on my right side and saw an unfamiliar being there. "Pleiadians," the being said, adding that the word was associated with where I'm going tomorrow. I was told to look this up. I heard the words: galactic, interstellar, star seed, light being; then the being put his hands near my heart and told me that I was embedded with healing energy and that I bring and radiate it wherever I go. I saw angels standing on one side of me and star beings on the other, all with their hands on my shoulders, supporting and guiding me.

After documenting these three experiences, I closed my eyes and tuned in to my Spirit team to ask about the repeated messages to allow in help. "I'm not aware of anyone yet who would able or willing to assist me," I said, "And I'm not even sure how they'd help anyway." No answer was received in that moment of asking, but I knew answers would come when the timing was right.

A short while later, as I was sipping coffee and looking at my computer, I was guided to pull up info on Devils Tower, which had been coming into my mind here and there for the past several weeks and always made me think of *Close Encounters*. This national monument in Wyoming is considered a sacred site with significant cultural and spiritual significance for more than twenty American Indian tribes, and has been the location of sacred religious ceremonies for centuries. This month was reported to be an especially significant time, as it correlated to summer solstice on June 21. *Ah!* I thought, recalling my dream, back on Day 60 in Lake Port, that specifically referenced that date.

Hmm, well, we would see how this all played out with the dates. I was still planning to follow my inspiration one day at a time, and right now, it seemed to be telling me to head toward Devils Tower tomorrow. I had felt strongly that the energy there would be powerful and healing and I was excited to experience it.

Then the third dream message flashed in my mind, instructing me to look up the word "Pleiadians." It was somehow connected to where I was going tomorrow, which was interesting as I had only just decided that! Now really curious to see if there was a connection, I googled "Pleiadians and Devils Tower" and I could not believe what I found!

*"The Kiowa tell the tale of a bear chasing seven maidens who are saved by the tower rising from the ground. However, instead of returning to their village, the girls ascend to the sky as stars, transforming into the **Pleiades, or "Seven Sisters," star cluster**— which, if you choose to visit Devils Tower at night, are clearly visible right above the monument during the fall."*[1]

[1] https://www.visitrapidcity.com/blog/2020/10/spirit-season-story-devils-tower-national-monument

This afternoon I enjoyed a wonderful spiritual healing training that included several guided meditations for attuning us to the physical and the spiritual worlds. At one point, I'd gone so deep into meditation that I lost consciousness! Again, Archangel Michael showed up for me and I felt him comforting me saying, "You can connect with us anytime. We're always here with you."

In our final meditation, I could feel myself receiving heart healing. Angels, their wings outstretched and connected, were encircling me and surrounding me with white light. I was told to allow myself to receive healing. I could sense myself releasing thoughts that had been bothering me and just handing them over to the angels to transform them for me.

It was an absolutely beautiful experience that I didn't want to end! Afterward, I felt sparkly, lighter, filled with positive energy. When I came back into my physical body and grounded myself, I looked outside of the nearby window and saw a couple of small feathers floating by!

After my class, I ran to the grocery store to pick up some items for dinner. Everyone I encountered was so nice and helpful, from the fellow shoppers to the cashier and the store manager.

The same was true when I went to grab an afternoon coffee. The young girl at the coffee shop was sweet and talkative with me. She even walked all the way from behind the counter to the other side of the shop to hand-deliver my coffee!

Between my spiritual healing with the angels and these beautiful people in the local shops, it looked as though I was already beginning to *accept help from those around me!*

# DAY NINETY

## Gillette, WY

It was hard to believe ninety days had passed since I began this trip, yet it also felt like much longer. One thing was for sure, I had established a routine for quickly packing up my things and getting ready to hit the road. Today, I had an eight-hour drive to Gillette, Wyoming ahead of me.

It was rainy out, and once on the highway I went through some pretty intense downpours and lightning storms where the visibility was really poor. Thankfully, each time I was guided out to safety, where there were blue skies again. The land here was absolutely beautiful! As I neared the exit for my hotel, the skies were looking dark again, so I put out a quick prayer to please hold the rain off until I arrived. The next thing I knew, I saw a huge rainbow in the sky as if a direct response to my request! Less than thirty minutes later I rolled up under the port cochere of my hotel, just as it started again. Talk about perfect timing!

I was really looking forward to going to Devils Tower the following day. With further research and reading, I discovered that the national monument and the Grand Tetons are considered energy vortices and sacred spiritual centers for the tribes inhabiting the areas. No wonder I was guided to both. On this spiritual journey, it certainly made sense that I'd be called toward the most powerful vortices and spiritual areas of the U.S.

# DAY NINETY-ONE

## Devils Tower, WY to Sioux Falls, SD

I was up even earlier than usual and by 5 a.m. had slipped out to grab a quick breakfast to go. The sunrise was beautiful to behold and it felt good to be out in the brisk morning air on empty streets while the world still slept.

After a short drive north, I arrived at Devils Tower and was pleased to find only a few people there. I decided to take one of the longer hiking trails that wound around the tower. On the hike, I saw multicolored prayer flags, left by various tribes, hanging from tree branches. I began offering my own prayers, asking for love, light, protection, and healing for my loved ones. I asked to receive whatever energy I was meant to receive from this sacred land. While continuing to walk and pray, I received this interesting download:

***Like nickel, which forms alloys with other metals to make it resistant to cracking under pressure, the mixing of your unique energy imprint with the energy of each vortex area blends making both you and Mother Earth stronger, more resilient.***

The message added to the increasing clarity about why I was being drawn to these vortex areas and sacred lands. Not only was I being healed and strengthened, I was meant to offer healing in return. I'd been naturally doing this all along, but it felt good to have more conscious awareness and understanding of it. As I continued walking, I asked to embed my own energetic imprint upon the land as an offering of healing to the Earth. I set the intention to channel divine healing energy through each of my steps on this sacred land.

On my way out, I saw a line of cars snaking up to the entrance of the park and thanked goodness for my early start. With a clear mind and a grateful heart, I hit the road and headed for Sioux Falls, roughly six hours away. There was something about these long drives that put me in a beautiful state of receiving downloads of inspiration and information, and today was no different. I recorded a ton of material for my upcoming talk for a group of Special Educators entitled "How to Cultivate and Maintain a State of Presence for Effective and Compassionate Communication."

As I crossed the border of Wyoming and South Dakota, I thought about the two worlds I was moving between. In one world, I was very left-brained, logical, and analytical, studying physics and speech pathology. I was following the practical path. In the other world, I was very right-brained, artistic, creative, empathic, spiritual, and intuitive.

For a long time I'd felt caught in the middle of these two sides as they battled each other for dominance. Now, I was finally finding a way to allow a blending without having to give up or deny one for the other. I was finally ready to integrate all these aspects of myself to bring my unique perspective and skill set to the world.

# DAY NINETY-TWO

## St. Louis, MO

The alarm went off at 5 a.m., tearing me from a deep sleep. Though I'd stirred once or twice during the night I had not gotten out of bed, which showed how tired I was. It was still dark out when I slid into the car for a breakfast run. My eyes were still glazed over from sleep, even after using eye drops. Luckily there was a Mickey D's just around the corner, so I didn't have to drive far.

There was one car pulling into the drive-thru in front of me, which I appreciated since it was so dark out and difficult to see where I was going. After placing my order I rolled up to the window and saw a middle-aged woman and a younger male employee scrambling to get everything together (even though there were only two of us in the line). I heard one say to the other that they "thought" they'd already made the coffee; then they paused to glanced worriedly at me before scrambling around the kitchen again. It was almost humorous, like watching a sketch comedy on tv.

In that moment, I had the thought to ground and then send comforting, loving energy to these two people. As I did so, I asked our teams of spirit helpers to please help them find their flow. I thought about suggesting that I move my car up ahead and park, but was given the next thought that "no, I can just wait right where I am, it'll be fine." It only took a few minutes before they had my order ready, no problem. It was a good reminder that no matter where I go, I can choose to make a difference and bring helpful and healing energy to each person and place I encounter, whether I'm at McDonald's or on sacred vortex land.

This reminder had come in perfect timing, as I was heading back East, the starting point of this venture. I was coming full circle and yet I really wasn't getting the sense that my trip would be done there. It would serve as just another waystation and a good resting point, like one of the times in life when things seem to pause even as our souls continue to evolve.

Funny, the name of the next place I was spending the night, in St. Louis, was called, "EARTH CITY." Also, St Louis, I'd recently learned, is known as "THE GATEWAY CITY" because of its access to transportation routes in all directions. It was more symbolism, this time of the many directions or routes I have taken already, and will take moving forward.

I got the nudge to check my oil last night and again this morning. Recalling the accuracy of that message last time I received it, I opened the hood and reached for the dipstick; sure enough, it was barely showing any oil! On my way out, I stopped at a gas station right across from the hotel and they had only two bottles left of the oil I needed. The total for both bottles: $12.12. Repeating numbers are powerful signs, so I looked up the meaning. The Universe was reminding me to trust in my intuitive guidance and the messages I was receiving.

It takes time and consistent training to not only hear and correctly interpret, but also to trust and follow through with those subtle nudges coming from a higher power help you. That said, it's up to us to do our part to help ourselves. For example, I was making sure to stop for gas more often, and keep a closer watch on my oil levels instead of asking for or relying on the Divine to help me when I was already in a pinch.

Across this leg of my trip, I'd been made aware of multiple and ongoing number sequences being shown to me. It was as though I was having a conversation via messages symbolized through these number sequences across the day. They would also give me a number sequence with a message containing the exact wording for something I saw on the road or heard in my audiobook. I was receiving signs and evidence to let me know that my guides were always with me and aware of what was happening around me.

I decided to spend one night in Asheville and then rendezvous at my parents' house in Fayetteville. I texted them today to make sure it was okay to arrive on Monday, though I didn't have to be psychic to know their answer. They are always welcoming.

Again, I had the sense of coming full circle, though I was certainly returning to Fayetteville a very different person than when I had left. It was hard to believe this stretch of my trip was coming to a close; there was so much more adventure and travel to come, but I was ready to give myself time for some comfort, peace, rest, rejuvenation, and support from people who love me and are always there for me. And it was perfect timing that I would be there on June 16 – my birthday!

## DAY NINETY-THREE

### Asheville, NC

Last night in my dream, Michael was doing a reading for me. He began calculating dates on a calendar saying that based on the alignment of the sun to the moon, ***"June 21st will be very significant for you."***

When I woke I heard an old Madonna song playing in my mind, specifically the line about her "having a tale to tell." I could feel Spirit's energy vibrating around me, like it was touching my arm to get my attention and tell me I needed to share my story as well. Interestingly, I had been thinking how the life I lead and the connection I have to Spirit would be unbelievable or "out there" to most people, from the conversations I have daily to the things I see/sense and have come to understand as the language of Spirit. A perfect example is the presentation I'd been asked to do for another special educator. She asked that I not use words like "meditation, mindfulness, or grounding" too much because they would probably be too woo-woo for the participants. If they only knew that those terms were part of my "normal people" vocabulary, and that they were just the tip of the iceberg of what I usually use!

On the flip side, I'd always thought it was crazy that some people don't realize that everything in the Universe, including us, is made of energy vibrating at different frequencies. If you believe that's woo woo, then you have to believe physics is woo woo, too! Some physicists are now acknowledging that our thoughts emit vibrational signals of varying frequencies and that this is how we can communicate and pick up information telepathically. Even Einstein called quantum physics' concept of entanglement "spooky action at a distance." As brave as Dr. Edgar's Mitchell was in exploring space, it took even more bravery to forge a spiritual path back here on Earth, especially in the face of criticism by colleagues.

Bottom line: I wasn't completely closed off to the idea of sharing my story, but I wasn't yet convinced that I should do it either.

CHAPTER FOURTEEN

# COMING APART

*"Now is the time to take separate paths. This is a sign to put an end to what is no longer working for you."*

**~Collette Baron-Reid,**
**The Enchanted Map Oracle Cards**

# DAY NINETY-FOUR

## Fayetteville, NC

As I traveled the stretch of road from Asheville to Fayetteville, my launching point ninety-three days earlier, I thought about the coming days with excitement. Yes, I would celebrate my birthday on June 16; however, I was more focused on June 21st – the date that had come up as significant in several messages from Spirit.

Also on my mind was the experience with the Madonna song and Spirit's nudge to share my story. I still wasn't sure I was ready to divulge such intimate details about my life, but I kept getting those signs and nudges. I came to two decisions: the first was that I would schedule an appointment with an editor for June 21st to learn about the process; the second was that I would tell my story only if it would be healing and inspiring to others, helping them find the courage to take the first step onto their own unique path and allow their gifts and talents to emerge. Most people aren't going to be psychics or mediums, of course, but we can ALL tap into our intuition more and part of my purpose is to support others on their journey.

I began thinking about how much I'd been inspired and supported throughout my own journey – my entire life, really – and how I wanted to pay this forward. I'd always held the belief that we come into this life with not just a Plan A, but an infinite number of backup plans that set ourselves up for support and success. These plans include perfectly timed synchronistic events to help us along the way and keep us moving in the right direction if we start to get off track. These events can be anything from being guided to an inspiring book to a chance encounter with people who offer insight at just the moment we need it to get us back on the path.

# DAY NINETY-FIVE

I woke at 7 a.m., the latest in months, then stayed in bed for my morning meditation before joining my parents downstairs. It sure was nice to "sleep in," and have someone cook me breakfast for once! I didn't feel rushed and I didn't have to be anywhere. There were a couple of healing groups I was scheduled to attend, but they weren't until later in the afternoon and I was excited about them.

After showering, and getting ready, I sat with the express intention to tap into my higher self and receive direct answers to specific questions. This was a change from my usual method, which was to tap in and allow whatever needed to come through. Today, I just felt called to try something different.

**Question #1** - Should I keep the meeting with this editor next week?

**Answer:** WAIT on this. You will be matched up. It's in the works!

**Question #2**- What book should I be working on?

**Answer:** This journey. (I then saw image of me walking along the road in Salt Flats as the book's cover.)

**Question #3** – What about the other book concepts?

**Answer:** NOT YET, those will come further down the road.

**Question #4** – Should I go to Lilydale and, if so, when?

**Answer:** Summer – July good.

**Question #5** – What else do I need to know/do that I didn't already ask?

**Answer:** Rest for now, you will be moving, learning, and practicing again soon.

I was elated to get such quick and specific responses, and excited to use this new system more for guidance!

## DAY NINETY-SIX

For most of my adult life, I'd gifted myself with a psychic reading for my birthday. This year, I set up an appointment with Pam, my mentor, a couple of days before my actual birthday.

Right away, my guides wanted to focus on "where" I was headed and described the importance of being in a place that was peaceful and surrounded by the beauty of nature. I needed to be in a place that would give me a sense of inner peace and upliftment for this next phase of my journey. She predicted it would be somewhere on the West Coast near access to both mountains and ocean. The message she shared was:

***This is a multifaceted incarnation for you.***
***You march to the beat of your own drum.***
***This multifaceted aspect of you that is emerging***
***is just the tip of the iceberg.***
***There will be a further cracking open or blossoming.***

*She was certainly spot-on with that message,* I thought as I recalled the "Coming Apart" oracle card I had pulled for myself that very morning. It gave the same exact message!

Pam continued, saying that this place would be temporary as I would continue to have the impulse to move to another "guidepost." I loved that she used this term because it reminded me of the "waystations" that were always described by my guides as well as by Michael. "Eventually you'll plant roots" she added, "but not right away." I asked her about Lilydale since I kept getting the inspiration to visit there, but she didn't get a good feeling about this location for me and said it was coming through as a "no."

She said that I was very strong, but that I still had a wound in my heart that needed to be healed. My guides shared: *"We want you to receive healing. Allow yourself to be in that surrendered state in order to receive healing."*

The next card she pulled was "Shame," which, she explained, referred to my heart wound. It was directly tied to my ex. "You need to work to release this," she added. I told her how in my meditation yesterday I'd felt the need to channel healing to him to help repair the pain I caused him. Immediately, Pam advised me to change my verbiage around this. "You have to stop telling yourself that you were the 'cause of his pain.' Of course he's hurt with the ending of the relationship. You were the one to speak the truth and it hurts to hear the truth. Now allow yourself to release judgment of yourself for doing what was right for you both."

A lot of divine healer cards came up, indicating the healing my guides were doing with me as well as the work I was pursuing to help others. Finally, Pam indicated that everything would be coming full circle for me with a time for celebration. The book I was guided to create would be completed once I found a place of stability.

## DAY NINETY-EIGHT

Happy Birthday to Me! I woke feeling tired, having tossed and turned several times during the night. It felt as though my guides were sharing golden nuggets of wisdom throughout my dreams. I quickly jotted down the few still running through my mind.

***Choose and act from a place of love.***
***Time for healing and rest.***
***Allow the natural unfoldment.***
***The power within you is just the tip of the iceberg.***

In my morning meditation, I received a visual of my guides cheering for me, like a celebration. I was told to stay positive because there was so much to look forward to. I received the knowing that I would be called to work on a book about this journey and that the right editor would be coming. The name "Transcendent Publishing" dropped into my mind. Just the other day I had received an email about a writing workshop with the owner of this company, who was working with Sunny Dawn Johnston! After the meditation, I pulled a card from Sunny's Multidimensional Oracle deck and received the Guardian Angel card, giving me a beautiful message of unconditional love and support, reminding me that I'm never alone.

Later in the morning I saw a missed call from Jared. He had also sent me a gift, but I had held off opening it and listening to his voicemail until after my therapy sessions. I was glad I did, because as I read his card and heard his kind and loving message, I started crying and couldn't stop. Then I opened the signed John Holland book he'd sent me – such a sweet gesture. Once again, feelings of guilt over any hurt I might have caused him rose up.

Five months had passed since I decided to leave my relationship and home, and though there had been much excitement on this new path, it had not been an easy one. If I was being honest, it had mostly been a roller coaster of emotions as I tried to find stability and purpose, with only my inner GPS to guide me. It had been working, for sure, but I still questioned myself and my decisions at times – even more so, it seemed, since returning here. I felt more uncertain about what I was doing and where I was going; I was also more judgmental of myself for the lack of clarity – like I should probably have a better idea by now!

**Sometimes the road home is a long, bumpy one.
It is challenging and you can't see where it leads you,
but somehow you just know and trust you'll end up
where you need to be.**

Funny, I'd never exactly had the best sense of direction, yet I somehow always ended up where I needed to go in the right timing. Now, I was counting on that more than ever.

# DAY NINETY-NINE

I was so grateful for Saturday circle today. Other than a few people in my life, no one yet knew I was doing psychic and mediumship work, so it was very important to be amongst like-minded individuals who were simultaneously working to develop individually while supporting one another. It was also, so important to continue putting in the work and discipline to hone my craft.

As usual, Pam talked to us about "coming out of the psychic closet," which is what I'd been thinking about more and more now. My website was ready and I'd even published it, only to immediately "unpublish" it the next day because I just didn't feel "ready" yet. Obviously, this was a hurdle I still need to clear.

Pam then paired us up and put us in separate breakout rooms to read each other. Not surprisingly, my partner delivered more messages about me putting myself out there. She described seeing the image of my face, then watched as it morphed into another face, indicating that there were two sides of me: one introspective and very protective, afraid to be seen, and the other was the one I allowed people to see. The message was, "You have built enough support and skill in the work you do and now it's time to show this side of yourself to the world."

# DAY ONE-HUNDRED-ONE

My sleep had been more restless the past of couple nights. I had the sense of being "up on the blocks," as if I was being worked on by my spirit team, which is exactly what I'd been asking for lately. I was badly needing some realignment!

Then, last night, I was given an interesting message in my dream. First, I heard the phrase, ***"As Above So Below,"*** followed by the written words appearing before me:

तन्त्र

***Don't follow the TANTRAS of others make your own.***

Interesting that they specifically used the Sanskrit term "tantras," which I'd only heard in reference to a sexual experience. Since I was pretty sure that wasn't where this message was trying to go, I did a quick google search and learned that tantra literally means "to loom, warp, weave" as in a "method, teaching, or practice." It appeared that the dream was trying to offer the following advice:

***Don't just follow the spiritual methods or practices of other teachers, weave your own. What you interweave into your teachings will reflect wisdom you're receiving directly from the Source.***

I'd noticed on this journey that I tended to feel most challenged when I focused on reaching some destination or trying to achieve some end result before the timing was right. Like a child wanting the toy or candy, I was having a tantrum because I couldn't get it "right now."

I just had to pause and remember that even on the days when I felt the most resistance, growth was still happening. I was always moving forward and going much faster than it seemed at the time. I needed to give myself ample time to integrate and "weave" everything into my daily life.

Today I received an email offering me a contract for summer school speech therapy services. What a blessing! Going week-to-week to different Airbnbs, not to mention all the driving around with crazy gas prices, wasn't the most budget-friendly way to travel.

Bottom line: I could have really used a break but I could use the cash in my bank account more. Now, not only would I be able to replenish my cash reserves, I would save a lot by staying with my parents for this extended visit. Things are truly always working out for me!

## DAY ONE-HUNDRED-TWO

It was going to be a full day, with online therapy sessions in the morning followed by a healing class. I got an early start and had a quick breakfast with my dad, then came upstairs to get ready and have some privacy. My parents are wonderful, and I'm grateful for the chance to visit with them and for their hospitality, generosity, and unconditional love, but I needed freedom to do my own thing. I planned to be here for another week or two, but I also needed to figure out my next steps.

After the healing class I had lots of paperwork and emails to contend with. I have to say, I don't love the rules, regulations, and procedural portion of the coursework, but it is necessary – something to get through so I can focus on what I love: the actual channeling of spirit energy to offer healing.

Every time I sat in the power and attuned with Spirit, I always felt an almost immediate connection. That connection was getting stronger and stronger and my vibration raised more and more. I loved that. It was something I could always trust in.

## DAY ONE-HUNDRED-THREE

### June 21st

Finally, the day had arrived, and I was not just referring to Summer Solstice – when the sun stands still in the sky – but the date I'd been told would somehow be significant for me. It started with me waking up crying from the following dream:

> *I'm sitting on a couch with Jared, watching a movie-like slideshow of our travel pictures. There are ten pictures in a row, each representing a different memory. I say we have one more Christmas ornament to put up on the tree, which we had gotten together on our last trip. This is our last night together. I say, "I'm going to really miss you," then I hug him and start crying my heart out.*

Through this Dream Healing, I was once again forced to face, and really feel, the last bit of sadness and enormous sense of guilt I'd been carrying. I'd thought I had cleared it, only for it to resurface on my birthday. Now, I could feel these deepest raw emotions, all the way to my core, being released. This dream was allowing me to finally bring closure.

In my morning meditation, I was shown the image of spiritual teacher Tom Cratsley, then guided to look at Lilydale again for an upcoming visit. I was being told by my higher self to follow my own intuition, rather than what others have told me. **"There is a reason you are guided to go,"** I was told. Tom's healing course was dropped into my mind with the message that **"it can all work out after all."** I was shown an image of myself at Lilydale doing healing work. I knew this practice would advance me a lot and that I would be using it moving forward. I saw myself bringing my study, knowledge, and experience of various healing techniques together in my own unique way.

I had been considering a week-long healing workshop of his but decided not to go when I realized it interfered with two of my other online healing class commitments. Then, while perusing the website and seeing names like Raymond Moody and Eben Alexander listed as mainstage speakers, I became excited about it again. This led to a casual search of places to stay in the area, when I came across a guesthouse owned by none other than ... drumroll ... Tom Cratsley!

Then, I received the message to relax more in the process:

***The less you resist the easier things will flow to you.***
***You're moving forward either way, but you might as well relax and enjoy the ride more. It won't be such a bumpy ride.***
***You've been holding on so tightly and resisting the flow.***

I was shown the image of someone who realizes they are going to crash or fall and tries to brace themselves, resulting in worse injuries than if they had just relaxed into the fall.

***Just relax and trust that you won't fall.***

This morning I received an email from Pam confirming the cancellation of our one-on-one mentorship appointment. The cancellation was at my request, as the session conflicted with a Past Lives workshop with Tony Stockwell I wanted to attend; however, I then started to analyze and question my choice. I sat down on the floor, closed my eyes, and visualized the thoughts quieting, then dropped down into my heart.

A bit later, I was able to feel and hear this guidance:

***There's no right/wrong or yes/no.***
***Don't keep wavering, going back and forth, questioning.***
***Just make a choice and then go with it.***
***Most importantly, don't seek out or follow other people's advice.***
***Make your own choice and then trust in it.***

This reminded me of the advice I'd previously received to be discerning about where I'm sourcing my information. My mind then went specifically to my birthday reading, in which I got a "no" to Lilydale that was counter to the inner calling I'd sensed for some time now. No matter who it's coming from, even a mentor, I needed to run the information through my own filter to determine if it resonated and was in alignment with the guidance I was receiving directly from Source. I had to trust that there was a reason I was being pulled there. The downloads kept coming:

*Remember to always trust in what YOU receive,*
*not what others receive for you.*
*The "advice" or readings interpreted and shared by others may serve as further confirmation of what you already know, but always be discerning about the info you are getting from others.*
*No one else knows what's best for you, better than you.*

Following the guidance coming from within, I chose to stick with my plan to attend the Past Lives workshop. I was so glad that I did! Not only did Tony share a plethora of wisdom with examples from his own readings and real-time demonstrations, he was hilarious, humble, and a wizard with his words. During breakout sessions, I had the opportunity to both give and receive wonderful readings today.

In the first reading given to me, a past life in Egypt came through. My partner described an "easier" life in which I balanced between work and time for rest and grounding. I also felt supported in my work, which encompassed psychic mediumship, past lives, and healing. "You were always ahead of your time," she said, "but you were respected in this life and sought after for your services." She then went on to explain why this life was showing itself to me now and how it could help me:

*It's telling you that it's time to resurrect those talents. You're at a fork in the road right now, which is symbolic of a change, taking a new path, and of all your different talents coming together.*

*You're being told to trust yourself and your abilities. Whenever you find yourself at a fork in the road, go back to your heart, ground yourself, and get quiet. You are in the midst of a significant shift in your soul's progression!*

In the second round of break-out readings, we did an exercise where we each shared a "block" that seemed to be holding us back in some way. Then we each took turns tuning in to describe a past life that related to this and offer some helpful guidance to help release the block. I requested information on why I felt resistant to "coming out" to others about my psychic and mediumistic abilities and received the following:

*The feeling of judgment and being vulnerable or exposed has caused you harm in past lifetimes and this pain is carried over into your present life. However, it's being worked on currently, it's being healed, and you will get past this. Keep peeling away the layers. Through your own healing work, you will be able to reciprocate healing for others and will share the knowledge you've gained.*

After we switched roles and I had conducted my reading for my partner, I received wonderful feedback that my messaging was so spot-on and helpful that I *had* to be doing this professionally already. As always, I was paired with the person I could best serve and who could best serve me. Her beautiful and kind feedback was the confidence boost I needed to republish my website later that evening. I was officially out there!

**Summer solstice:**
**Associated with new beginnings, a time of transition and powerful healing.**

Though not at all in the way I had anticipated, June 21st had most definitely been significant for me. The events of the day had led to an emotional transformation that left me feeling so much more trusting, connected, confident, re-energized and clear-minded.

I felt better than I had in a while and I felt like, once again, I had a plan moving forward.

CHAPTER FIFTEEN

# THE ILLUSION OF ENTRAPMENT

***"Your belief that you are trapped is an illusion. If you let go of your insecurities and your absolute focus on the challenges you face, opportunities for freedom will reveal themselves."***

**~Radleigh Valentine,**
**Angel Wisdom Tarot**

# DAY ONE-HUNDRED-FOUR

Today was the second and final day of the Past Lives workshop. I was fully engaged in Tony's discussion when, about ten minutes in, Zoom froze up, then shut down completely. At first, I thought it might have been a technical issue on his end, but after a few failed attempts to rejoin the room, I realized the Wi-Fi in the house had gone out!

I knew immediately that it was Spirit, forcing me to take a break from the computer so They could work on me. You see, just prior to class, I had questioned whether I should attend because I felt burned out and tired. Moreover, I had felt such powerful healing work being done on me in my morning meditation that I kept wishing I could go back into another meditation and rest. When I didn't follow this subtle knowing of what I truly needed, Spirit took action on my behalf!

I promptly closed down my laptop, walked into the privacy of my bedroom, and laid down on the bed for my pre-arranged spiritual tune up. There, I received both energy renewal and loving messages of encouragement.

Later, after a fun night with my parents, I was getting ready to climb into bed when I realized I was feeling emotional, sad, and even angry. I put on some sound bowls for healing and fell asleep to this.

During the night I continued the releasing physically. My body went through spells of being hot and sweating to cold chills. I requested healing from my spirit team and was given the understanding that I was going through another "upgrade" and the current work being done on me involved an overhaul of my whole system. This major transformation meant more emotions coming up, the releasing of negative thought patterns, some physical symptoms, and an overall heightened sensitivity.

It felt overwhelming, but I just allowed myself to feel what I was feeling. I knew it was part and parcel to this ongoing healing and shedding process, and that I was leaving more layers behind.

## DAY ONE-HUNDRED-FIVE

This morning, I connected before getting out of bed. I took the time to envision and set the intention for what I wanted in all areas of my life: love, relationships, work, creative projects, health, etc.

Knowing that this flow of energy was inspired by Spirit, I just went with it. At the end of my conscious verbalizing of my desires and intentions to Spirit, I was shown the image of a genie and a magic carpet. I was told over and over...

**AND SO IT IS**
**AND SO IT IS**
**AND SO IT IS**

In desperate need of some grounding and physical activity, I signed up for a hot yoga class. Since it was my first time at the studio, I arrived thirty minutes before class, allowing ample time to check in without being hurried. It was perfect timing, because the teacher was just about to start her 5:30 class and let me into the waiting room before locking the door.

I had the place to myself for a bit and saw the perfect book to keep me occupied as I waited: Louise Hay's *Heal Your Body: The Mental Causes for Physical Illness and the Metaphysical Way to Overcome Them.* I had always deeply resonated with Hay's own story of sexual trauma and how this had later shown up as cancer in her body, which she was able to heal through alternative methods, just as I had done in 2017.

I felt so good throughout class, sweating my ass off and loving every moment of it! At the end, the teacher provided refreshing, cold wet towels and a beautiful mix of essential oils that she massaged for each of us. We'd done the asana part and now would get to the "real" purpose of yoga and my favorite part ~ Savasana शवासन ~ which means SURRENDER!

I had so needed to get off the computer and back into a routine of grounding and physical movement... back out into the world again. I was reinvigorated!

## DAY ONE-HUNDRED-NINE

Last night before bed, I had set my intentions to clearly remember and correctly interpret my dreams so I could understand the information in a way that helped me in my waking state. I had also asked for help from my team to clear anything that no longer served me.

When I woke up, I recalled a significant dream in which I was trying to close and lock the door to my new apartment, but I couldn't no matter what I did. I was annoyed and a little bit worried that someone or something would come in. This was a reoccurring theme that had been showing up in my dreams since I was a young child. Then, when I started to move into a waking state, I saw a flashing light with different moving shapes within it. It felt "off" and appeared to be representative of my misaligned energy.

In the past, I had always assumed this recurring dream of not being able to lock the door was directly related to the trauma of seeing neighbors physically attack my mother when I was a young child. About a year ago, however, I began to question this after having another version of this dream, one that symbolized me keeping my true self out, and my unconscious and conscious fear of letting others in, revealing myself to them, and giving up my privacy. The message here was that there was really nothing to fear in opening the door.

Since it came up again in my dreams last night, I was obviously still in process of releasing this. At least this dream was set in a new place and much less volatile and fear-based than it had been in the past. Definitely an improvement!

Afterward, I went downstairs to say hello to my parents and chat for a little before getting ready for yoga. My mom said there was something outside that she wanted to show us. I looked and saw it was a huge moth – bigger than any I'd ever seen – on the wall just outside the door to the deck. As I believe moths often represent visits from our loved ones in spirit, I immediately thought it might have been drawn here because of the spiritual work I'd been doing and the energy I was bringing.

That evening, as my parents and I enjoyed a delicious Korean dinner, Mom randomly started talking about several "weird dreams" she'd had in the past. They seemed like premonitions, she said, including one before her mother passed many years earlier. What?! I loved that she was sharing that out of the blue and to discover that our gifts run in the family!

She then shared some sad news she'd heard earlier that day: a good friend of hers had passed away the previous week. I told her that the moth outside, which she'd been looking at again when I got home from yoga, was probably her friend visiting her to say hello. Mom smiled, seemingly touched by that thought, and I was glad to have brought her comfort.

I then asked my mom to tell me more about her father's side of family. She shared that my great-grandmother (who, like me, is a Dragon in the Chinese zodiac) was a healer in her village in Korea, administering all kinds of herbal and alternative modalities, including acupuncture. I had sensed this and even heard in past readings that this particular relative also had "the gift." Mom went on to remind me of her cousin, who also had a premonition in her dream of a "divorce." She even called my mom to ask if my parents were splitting up. "Of course not," my mom had replied, laughing off the ridiculous notion. However, a week later, I was bunking in the guest room because I'd left my relationship and my mom realized that the "divorce" involved me. It felt so validating to know that I was not as "weird" or different as I'd always felt, but had actually inherited a legacy.

I very much appreciated all this coming out now. It was perfect timing to give me more confidence and confirmation about my own path. For months, I'd been on the road, going to new places almost every week... always on the go and always in new unknown places by myself. Staying with my parents these past few weeks had been so helpful, affording me a safe space for rest, replenishment, healing, and releasing.

## DAY ONE-HUNDRED-TWELVE

I woke several times during the night, recalling some wisdom that was shared through my dreams:

*By giving attention to your journey NOW*
*You are able to change and positively affect the PAST.*

This seemed to refer specifically to karma from past lives as well as the healing I was doing of past experiences within this life.

After an easy day of online therapy sessions, I had a productive one-on-one mentoring session with Pam. She offered her usual abundance of helpful wisdom, then said she felt my psychic and medium work was accelerating very quickly. It was time, she said, to assign me some practice clients – the step before pushing me to get listed in the Psychic Directory! By this point, I knew that this journey was what really cracked my psychic gifts wide open. It was a powerful combination of the daily discipline to attune myself and develop a more intimate relationship with my guides and the all-day, everyday reliance on my intuitive skills to guide me, plus the vortex areas that enhanced and expedited the whole opening.

# DAY ONE-HUNDRED-THIRTEEN

I got off to a pretty early start this morning so I could prepare myself for mediumship circle. It would have been nice to sleep in but, as usual, our group practices made the sacrifice well worth it.

Pam had one member give a platform reading, and the spirit communicator who came through appeared to be one of my paternal great-grandfathers who was a naval captain. Since I'd been home, my dad had been letting me use his office every day to conduct my sessions. Sitting at his desk, I was surrounded by family memorabilia such as framed documents, our family tree, and old photographs – including that of my great-grandfather. It made sense, then, he was coming through with some sage advice, which was as follows:

*"The Sea is so vast,*
*but with a compass you'll always find your way."*

So perfectly said!

After class, I had plenty of time to sit for meditation and a little automatic writing for inspiration and guidance:

*You are a powerful creator.*
*Visualize and set clear intentions.*
*When you are wishy-washy, it slows the creation*
*from coming forward.*

*You are allowing fears and worries to come up*
*through your dreams at night, when you're least resistant*

*to the process. We are hoping to clear these out of your subconscious. Allow this to continue to happen in the night and, even better, set the intention to give us permission to do so.*

*We are working on your behalf, but it's much stronger when you intend. Be clear about your intentions.*

*Then just rest and take time for yourself. There will be more transformation coming soon. We are getting you ready for your upcoming trip.*

*CONTINUE TO ALLOW THE MAGIC TO FLOW TO YOU AND THROUGH YOU.*

## DAY ONE-HUNDRED-FOURTEEN

It was hard to believe I was leaving in just five days. I was already getting excited for the next phase of my adventure, eager to see what was in store for me on the road ahead. Time sure does fly!

After sleeping until 8 a.m., a rare treat, I meditated then pulled a tarot card: Ten of Earth, a very positive card indicating a time of completion and security in my near future. The card also spoke to honoring family traditions and passing on knowledge to the world. The message: "There's a strong emphasis on family lineage." This reminded me of the enlightening conversation I'd had with mom this past week about the psychic and intuitive sensitivities on her side of the family. The card also reflected finding peace, contentment, and stability in a place I could call home for myself.

That evening my parents and I watched *Hitchhiker's Guide to the Galaxy,* Which was hilarious and took me back to my dream the previous month It was in that dream that I received the date June 21 and the subsequent awareness of the repeated 2121 number meaning that "thoughts are like seeds that are about to sprout." The word "untethered" was once again coming to mind. Remembering this, I had the feeling that it was about time to get back on the road.

## DAY ONE-HUNDRED-SIXTEEN

I woke up at 6:30 a.m. still tired; this, despite sleeping hard and a nice long nap the afternoon before. I had been exhausted lately, and yesterday felt under the weather, but I knew it was a side effect of all the healing and releasing work being done. The physical symptoms had been more prominent since my healing sessions were amped up, and in fact I could feel focused healing energies on me, not just in the night but while meditating as well.

I recalled having many meaningful dreams last night and immediately proceeded to document and analyze them to uncover the messages coming through for me today.

DREAM #1
I'm in an office building and have to carry up some large pieces of furniture all by myself. I do it, and the wheels on the desk make it easier to get them into the room they need to be in; however, later I need to take them back down to my car but can't remember the exact door I came in. I'm trying to figure out the way before I start moving anything; I'm also not sure how I'll manage it all. I think I should start with two chairs and make sure it's the right way. Someone asks how I got all this up here and I say that the wheels helped.

MESSAGE:
I am anticipating a big job I have ahead of me and I'm feeling unclear and uncertain about whether or not I'll be able to manage it all on my own through all the ups and downs, though the dream shows me that

I am capable. I'm in the planning stages and will be moving forward again soon.

<u>DREAM #2</u>

I'm in some city in another country. It's daytime and warm. I see a motorcycle pass with a mother and two babies and I'm worried for them; no protective gear… and babies on a motorcycle? Later I see this mom and her husband upstairs in a very luxurious apartment and they have a line of people waiting to visit them.

The babies are now much bigger and they're all sitting down to eat. The mom says that when babies are bigger they get hungry faster and will cry and ask for food. As I'm leaving, a lady in line tells me that the mother inside has a famous family history or lineage.

<u>MESSAGE:</u>

I'm feeling protective of my creative projects (or "babies"). I feel worried about them taking off. This dream has to do with growth and how the bigger something gets, the faster the momentum and the more you need to "feed it." I feel like it's telling me I need to "feed" or give attention, energy, and focus to my writing, teaching, etc. because they are "hungry" for my attention (Note: While typing this I saw a blue light flash in the room, which for me is always a sign of confirmation from Spirit). The luxurious setting indicates that these projects will be successful, prosperous, and well-received as symbolized by the long line of people outside who want to see them. This also relates to gifts I'm carrying forward in my family lineage.

<u>DREAM #3</u>

I'm outside and it's nighttime and I'm trying to go to my hotel room in this strange city. Suddenly, the lights go out. I walk upstairs, find my room, and put away some things in a cabinet. I want to organize the room, but there's so much stuff there, cluttered. I'm tired and I go to lock the door but see it's a strange system. I figure out how to lock it, but I realize that the door is wide open on top and anyone can just climb right over and get inside my space if they want to, so the lock on the door is pointless. I think, "Well, that's a shitty system!" Then I'm made aware of a painting hanging on the wall, depicting the view outside my room. The trail ahead appears to be desert, but there is also some lush vegetation and I hear a voice that says, "The rain helps it to grow."

MESSAGE:

I'm feeling in the dark and lacking clarity, but that could also be a play on words indicating that I need more rest (ie. "lights out"). The hotel room symbolizes a temporary place. There is also the repeated theme of trying to lock and keep people out from coming into my space and realizing there's no way to do this.

I'm being shown my path ahead, which seems desolate and empty, hence the appearance of the desert landscape, but is actually rich and full of growth.

As I typed the dream meaning, I found my fingers being guided and the following download being delivered to me:

*When you view your life, your path, your own growth, you don't always see the richness of what is there and what is coming. You have been holding onto things from your past that need to be released. It's time to let go of the fear that you need to stay hidden or try to keep things and people locked out. There are some things that are out of your control, so just let them go. The rain symbolizes the emotional release you are allowing in now, which will help you grow and create abundance as you move forward in your life and on your path.*

**On the other side of the door that you keep trying to lock is your path, your purpose, Divine help, and so much growth and abundance just waiting for you.**

**~LET IT IN~**

This dream reflected my attempt to control and prevent the outer world from seeing the inner world that I experienced, the world I really lived in and embodied. It was very sacred to me, and I protected it and kept it apart from or hidden from others and was still struggling with the idea of letting them into this space. I have always had a firm boundary and divide here, but now I was being shown that it was time to release this.

***You can't stop it anymore as it's part of your path to open up and be more public, to reach, teach, and share about your own life experience and knowledge you've gained, which you will continue to channel and share.***

## INDEPENDENCE DAY

It was the Fourth of July, an irony that was not lost on me, as I was feeling the need for my own freedom and independence. I loved my parents, but I needed my own space. I do not like being hovered over, even when my parents are just being amazingly supportive and helpful. Plus, since we're all independent, strong-willed people, we sometimes butt heads over absolutely nothing.

At breakfast, I inquired more about our family ancestry and various details about my deceased relatives so when they come up in readings I could identify the evidence more accurately. Problem is, my parents don't know a whole lot about the details. They know a lot more than the average person about their family because my dad has done quite a bit of research; yet many things remain a mystery and my parents got a little defensive about it when I asked. It was so silly, really, because I just wanted to know what they DID know, not what they didn't know and why.

Sometimes, when you notice things heating up, the best thing to do is move away from the situation and allow the feelings to cool. It reminds me of the saying often used by people on a spiritual journey: "If you think you're enlightened, try spending a few days with your family!" In other words, everything you think you've learned will be put to the test because no one knows how to push our buttons more than the people who have been around us the longest!

After finishing breakfast, I quickly removed myself to go upstairs and realign my own energy, which was obviously triggering those around me too. It was just a sign that I was ready to venture off on my own again. The past few weeks had been a welcome respite that allowed me to replenish my funds and my energy and also spend some wonderful quality time with my parents, but it was about time to prepare for another launch.

After spending the afternoon shopping with my mom, I looked up some possible routes for my drive to New York since I would likely split the trip. The path that was shortest and seemed my best option went through West Virginia. Total time: eleven hours and one minute – 111! I'll take that as a good sign!

That night, my folks and I celebrated the Fourth with grilled burgers and the movie *Ford vs Ferrari* – which I love and they'd never seen before. My mom was so into the racing she was cheering on Ken Miles (played by Christian Bale). Spoiler alert: near the end of the film, Ken dies in a fire, and as I watched the scene I felt my heart pounding out of my chest. It was the same feeling I get when Spirit is connecting with me, and I felt that either Ken Miles or Carroll Shelby was blending with me in that moment. Afterward, I was so pumped, just as I was the first time I saw the movie. It took me back to my forty-fourth birthday, when Jared took me to the Barber Motorsports Parkway and we were trained by world-class drivers! It was such an amazing experience that I'll always cherish. God, I loved driving stick and I loved driving fast ... and not just fast, but with precision and control and being able to direct and focus the power.

It's an intense and amazing feeling and those Le Mans drivers are like superheroes to me!

The feeling of blending and my heart racing during the movie also reminded me of watching *Bohemian Rhapsody* for the first time. At the end scene of the Live Aid concert, I almost jumped up right there in the middle of the theater to cheer, shout, and sing along as if I was actually playing in a concert! I felt a powerful energy – similar to the blending that happens during my mediumship sessions – and it felt as though Freddie Mercury himself was connecting with me to view the scene through my eyes. It was so intense and another experience I will always remember.

## DAY ONE-HUNDRED-SEVENTEEN

Woke this morning at 5:55, a sign of pending changes and transformation, and got up to record the following dream:

*I am taking out the trash and it's nighttime. I'm feeling worried about something. I walk through some woods nearby toward a grove of trees and see the full moon shining from above and a gathering of magical butterflies, fireflies, and fairies. I pray to God over and over to please help me release my worry and fear and let go of anything that's not helpful to me.*

When I wake, I know I need to drop out of my head and into my heart. I need to release negative thoughts and feelings like worry and fear and just focus on what I want. I received the following advice over and over:

**"TRUST IN YOURSELF."**

**MESSAGE:**

I need to "take out the trash," or clean up my thoughts and feelings of worry, ask the Divine for help in this healing and clearing, and know that I'm being helped at night. I'm reminded of a previous dream in which I was told that there's "magic" happening at night on my behalf to transform me (represented by the butterflies).

I had a nice quiet breakfast on my own while my parents were getting ready for their own morning appointments. I kept asking and intending for my guides to please help me release and transmute any negative thoughts or feelings that I was still carrying around. I also did a healing meditation with a focus on my solar plexus for improved confidence in myself and my situation. I felt this area swirling and vibrating with strong energy and knew the work was happening. I kept repeating the affirmation given to me from my dream to help me focus on what I wanted and to seal it in and maintain this positive momentum.

**"TRUST IN YOURSELF."**

In the afternoon, as I did some packing and organizing in preparation of my upcoming travels, I came across a tarot deck made by Kymberley, my friend in Sedona with whom I'd had two healing sessions. I was inspired to pull a card for myself.

While standing by my bed shuffling the cards, I felt my legs and body vibrating. I recalled Kymberley saying how she had infused the cards with a very high vibrational energy. ***"They are a map to the higher timelines of existence and a bridge into other dimensions of realities…"***

When the vision paintings are combined with the interpretations, they intensify the personal energetic shift.

***"(They) are available for those seeking to change their lives… (and) are a succession of levels of awareness with related clearings and healings."***

Perfect! No wonder I was drawn to them on this day.

The card I pulled was
**THE WAY SHOWER: Sacred Path Blessings**

The description for this card and its Spiritual Mastery Quest was "I AM see-king my Sacred Spiritual Path and Gifts."

Every now and then I'd been hearing in my head "More Human Than Human," an oldie but a goodie by White Zombie, a favorite band from my high school days.

We are so much more than this human body; there is so much beyond this physical experience that most people don't see, sense, or realize at all. The songs reminds me how different my everyday world is, how very, very strange and unbelievable it would seem to the average person.

There were many times over the last few weeks – especially over this last week – that I thought I'd "come out" to my parents about my psychic and mediumship work. Yet I always hesitated and stopped myself from opening up. I felt it would a) freak my mom out (she scares easily); b) my dad would joke about it; and c) at the end of the day I didn't know if there was any real purpose or need to share it.

Sometimes it's good to hold something sacred close to your chest until the timing is right. I was reminded of a quote by Jerry Hicks: ***"Keep your ideas to yourself until they are fully developed."*** Indeed, this felt like the best way to give myself freedom from what they thought and keep myself in alignment, so I decided to wait until I was more stable on my path before sharing with them.

## DAY ONE-HUNDRED-EIGHTEEN

Today was my last full day in Fayetteville, and I was ready to move on. Ready for movement, ready for new, ready to step out again and have my own space.

After waking, I lay in bed for my morning meditation and the following phrases flooded into my mind:

*You will lead and teach (this was repeated several times);*
*You will show others the path*
*And we will show you the way too*
*(111 flashed before me).*

Afterward, I started to look up meanings for 111 on my phone but was instead guided to close my eyes again and receive the meaning from my higher self…

**New beginning**
**Oneness**
**Leave the past behind, time to move forward on the path**
**Leadership**
**Let go of worry**
**You are a powerful manifestor**

The downloading of messages continued:

*You are worried that you can't carry the weight that's been handed to you… this responsibility. However, you were chosen for this life path and you can handle it and you will excel. You will continue to teach and help show the way to others, which will enable them to progress faster than they could without this guidance, just as you were able to do for yourself. You are a leader, teacher, an explorer, and someone who is not afraid to take needed risks that many others won't take. You will be supported and guided along the way.*

**THE SEA IS VAST, BUT YOU WILL BE GUIDED.**

*Radical change is needed*
*but it starts from within, not outside of ourselves.*

***Everyone is looking outside of self and blaming others for problems.***

***Instead, ask yourselves: "What are YOU doing to make positive change?"***

**CHANGE MUST START FROM WITHIN.**

## DAY ONE-HUNDRED-NINETEEN

The journey continues!

Last night, my parents and I enjoyed a wonderful Korean feast of all my favorite dishes. My mom made this especially for me since there aren't too many Korean food options on my travels.

Afterward, we sat down to watch *The Glass Castle,* a movie based on Jeanette Walls' memoir that I'd heard about the other day. It was the perfect thing for me to watch since I was working on my own memoir. Throughout the night, I'd felt the presence of Spirit with me, feeling a twitch in my eyebrow and seeing the spark of a blue light every now and then. While watching the movie, I also realized that two of the major locations in the movie are the same ones I'd be heading to: West Virginia and New York! Another perfect synchronicity and sign as confirmation of this Divine orchestration always happening on my behalf.

When I went upstairs to get ready for bed, I thought how brave Jeanette was to write and publish her story, including so many intimate details of her childhood and family life. It reminded me that although I was such a private person and always had been, I was now willing to share my own experiences if it would be helpful to others. I recalled when as a college sophomore I gave a presentation to one of my classes to raise awareness about sexual assault on campuses. I spoke about what exactly constitutes rape, since it had happened to me the year before at a dorm party with a complete stranger. It was very uncomfortable to reveal such a raw and traumatic experience to a class I barely knew, but if it would prevent it happening to one other person I was more than willing.

Last night, while getting myself ready for bed, I had stopped to look at myself in the mirror and say, “I’m ready for the next step.”

Once I climbed into bed, though, I did have that old all-too-familiar feeling of uncertainty; this lead to a quick rush of fear that bubbled up with a burst of tears as I tried to think of what I’d be doing for the next few months. I just let myself sit in this uncomfortable emotion, then watched as it passed through me like a rainstorm. I asked all the unseen angels, healers, helpers, and guides to please come be with me and give me comfort in this moment. I immediately felt a cold rush of air on my side that lingered for a moment. I thanked them for their quick response to my request, which brought me some comfort in knowing that, no matter what I was going through, I wasn’t alone.

## ON THE ROAD AGAIN

As I drove away from Fayetteville, I saw many synchronicities and signs, including the 9999 on my odometer which flipped right back to the number 1 for this trip, indicating a fresh start.

In fact, I saw multiple number ones along my drive. I knew this was also a reminder to check my thoughts and make sure I was focused on the positive. I had been a little testy this morning when my parents were trying to do a really nice thing but, rather than helping, they were really getting in my way and slowing me down. This is a pet peeve of mine, and once I’m in go mode I can get annoyed pretty easily if someone gets in my way or tries to slow me down – especially if they’re trying to tell me I should do something differently, as if they know better. But I felt really badly about the way I’d snapped at my parents and was wishing I could go back and redo that moment.

Just as I was thinking this, my reading with Michael earlier that year popped into my head. He had predicted that I'd likely find myself snapping at people (if I wasn't doing so already). I'd always been the peacemaker for everyone around me, but my guides had taken away my patience chips so I wouldn't continue putting up with situations that weren't working any longer or weren't good for me. That explained a lot, because I'd been completely unlike my usual self with Jared – we were fighting all the time and I couldn't stop myself from speaking my mind, even if I'd wanted to.

Now that flash came through, as if something similar might've been the case during my stay with my parents. If so, the annoyance I felt wasn't entirely bad because I needed the motivation and kick in the pants to get me back on the road, back onto my journey doing the work. I had needed the rest for a time, but I wasn't meant to get too comfortable either. There was more work to be done and it was time to get a move-on. I didn't need to be so hard on myself as there was a greater plan behind it... though I'd be sure to be sweeter to my folks next time because they don't deserve anything else.

As I was driving out the phrase "chasing rainbows" kept coming to mind. It made me think back to 2017, when I was in and out of the hospital and forced to focus my energy on regular daily prayer and meditation – and as a result I was given a ton of support. For much of the time, I was unable to walk or move much due to weakness and extended ongoing healing from surgery after surgery. The only walking I did for a while was from the couch, where I slept, to the half bath on that same floor.

When I could finally drive my manual car again – this took a good while because I had to regain enough strength in my legs to press the clutch and in my arm to change gears – I would take myself for drives around town. It was such a treat to be moving again and gain back a small sense of independence and freedom. I especially loved when it had rained because that meant I might see rainbows. I would drive all around just to find one and, if I did I'd stay on that road to follow it and keep it in my sights as long as

I could. There was a stretch of time where I would see so many rainbows, sometimes right over my townhome! I needed to believe in and experience some magic in my life because everything else was so overwhelming and huge, weighing me down. I did everything I could to look for, focus on, and milk any little bit of hope and happiness I could find.

I knew that was my team of angels, healers, and helpers, surrounding and supporting me, trying to heal and comfort me during this time. The rainbows were one simple way to uplift my spirits and they would always be a wonderful sign of this connection for me. And, of course, as I was driving out, I looked down at my phone and saw a spectrum of light being reflected, just like a rainbow!

CHAPTER SIXTEEN

# FATED MEETING

***"You are coming to a very important relationship in your life. Karma from past lives may have brought you together... (for) an important purpose that you hold."***

**~Sharon Anne Klinger and Sandra Anne Taylor, The Akashic Tarot**

# LILYDALE, NY

## PAST LIVES

Today was a wonderful start to the week-long Healing Mastery Training at Lily Dale's historic Healing Temple. I felt there was a significant and powerful reason that this particular group had gathered in this place at this time, and I was extremely excited to add my unique flavor and energy to the pot.

Our instructor, Tom, repeated exactly what my guides had told me: we would not only be giving healing but receiving a lot as well. I loved how we were able to dive right in and get a ton of hands-on practice. This was my kind of workshop!

With my first partner, I placed my hands very lightly on her shoulders and felt energy flowing from all directions into me. Suddenly – pow! – visuals started flooding in. I saw water rushing through my crown and down, then channeled straight into her heart, which is where I sensed she most needed healing. In my mind's eye I saw the word LOVE flowing to her and could feel a calming, soothing energy surrounding her.

Afterward, she said my right hand on her shoulder felt super heavy, though she knew I was barely touching her. That shoulder had been bothering her and she felt this was where a good bit of healing was being directed. I sensed the "weight" of my hand and discomfort was allowing her to feel and release the burden she'd been carrying on her shoulders.

While working with my second partner, I felt double the healing energy flowing through me to her. Again, I received lots of visual imagery, which is how I often interpret energy. I set the intention to connect with her higher self and saw her before me with eyes beautifully sparkling and glowing. I saw the energy flowing to our heart centers, becoming different colors that then turned into a sunflower. A beam of light flooded in from above, through her crown chakra all the way down to her heart. A swirling helix made of crystal appeared and was spinning as it moved down through her core, recalibrating her entire body. When I tapped in to see if there was any area that needed extra care, the heart appeared first, then her feet or lower legs, and I was told she had difficulty walking at times. She later confirmed issues with her left knee and foot, making it difficult to walk and robbing her of a beloved activity – hiking.

At the end, I saw a blue butterfly, symbolizing the completion of her healing and transformation, fly out of her heart. She confirmed that she also saw a blue light and felt the healing, mainly in her heart area – wonderful validations of what I had seen and interpreted. I was just loving the way this healing process was working, with me fully tapping into all my senses, especially my third eye and visual imagery.

Then it was time to switch. As she placed her hands on my shoulders and back, I could see/sense winged angels in white behind us, with their hands there too to offer healing. More joined us and formed a healing circle around me, offering love, comfort, and healing. It was beautiful. At the end I saw light and angel feathers falling upon me, then blue butterflies take off from my heart to indicate my transformation was complete.

That evening we returned for the second part of our Day 1 healing. I had beautiful readings – a combination of psychic and mediumistic – with three different partners, for the express purpose of heart-centered healing. The flow of information was accurate, specific, and intimate for everyone. One of my partners offered such heartfelt and appreciated encouragement, saying she felt proud to have met me because she sensed I would be doing very important work to inspire others. I could say the same for her and everyone else in the group! Like attracts like, and I was amongst leaders, teachers, and healers here.

Later, as we closed up for the night, I chatted with one of my partners. When she asked if I'd attended Tony Stockwell's recent Zoom on past lives, I drew back in surprise.

"Yes, wow, were you in that class too?!"

She said no, then pointed to a young man I hadn't formally met or worked with yet.

"He was in it and he said he saw you there!"

At that moment I realized I had seen him share in Stockwell's class. How crazy that he remembered me, especially since I had never commented and there were probably over fifty people there.

When I arrived back at my rental, the face of the young man flashed in my mind again. I wondered what would come of this connection. Then, as I was getting ready for bed, a thought popped into my head that stopped me in my tracks. The Past Lives workshop had happened on June 21 – the same date I'd been told repeatedly in my dreams to watch for because something significant would occur. Whoa! Talk about a divinely orchestrated synchronicity! My time at Lilydale had started off in an even bigger and better way than I had imagined, and I couldn't wait to see what tomorrow would bring!

## THE BRIDGE

On Day 2, I was paired with Farshad, the young man from the Past Lives class! I saw a beautiful, bright blue light, then sat back and channeled healing energy as a whole movie played out before me.

I saw his higher self smiling back at me, eyes sparkling, then the blue light expanded into a variety of colors, as if he had a prism reflecting light all around him. I heard the words "teacher" and "bridge," then saw him facing an expanse as a bridge, made of this prismatic light and various shapes, formed in front of him. It reminded me of the movie *The Last Mimzy*.

I was told that Farshad was a bridge between Earth and other realms and would be creating this connection through his presence and as a teacher. At the end of the healing, I saw him dressed in white robes with his hands in prayer as if thanking me and telling me our session was complete. Right after I saw this, I heard Tom say, "You'll know the healing is done when you see the colored lights become white." Exactly!

Interesting, I thought. Farshad, had a connection to other realms and I'd been continuously receiving information about the same thing over the past few months.

My amazement deepened when I asked him how he knew I was in the Past Lives class. He told me that was his first psychic or mediumship development class, and as he scrolled through the "classroom" he felt my energy through the screen! Clearly, there was some cosmic connection between us – and how perfect that we connected on the Summer Equinox, marking a time of new beginnings, and in a class on PAST LIVES, of all places!

Just as my multiple dreams had predicted: *"June 21st will be very significant for you."*

## VOLUNTEERING AT THE HEALING TEMPLE

After performing a healing session on Tom, he gave his official approval for me to volunteer my services as a Spiritualist Healing Trainee for the remainder of my time there. It was such a great learning experience. When I arrived on my first evening, there was already a small group of people in the pews, ready to receive healing. Another seven healers were at the front of the temple, attuning to Spirit through meditation.

The first man assigned to me smiled and identified the areas he wanted to focus on. After a short prayer, I stood behind him and placed my hands lightly on his shoulders. Immediately, I felt powerful energy streaming through me. Also, my attention was automatically drawn to the same areas the man had mentioned, as if Spirit was answering his specific request. Afterward, the man thanked me, saying that he could really feel the effect of the healing energy. He added that when he first saw me he somehow knew he was going to end up in my chair, and he was glad he did.

The next person had such a sweet, kind energy; she asked me to focus on her back. During the healing session, I could sense angelic presence around her and support with the healing. She seemed so peaceful and light when she left.

After the crowd was gone, we just sat and waited in meditation for the remainder of time. I sensed Spirit was helping me (and I'm sure everyone else, too) so I could receive healing as well. I was actually pretty tired and felt the beginning of a mild headache, so the time to rest and receive in this sacred space was appreciated.

## SPIRIT ORCHESTRATION

Our healing class today involved sound healing, something Tom said he didn't usually teach in this course but sensed this group was ready for something more advanced. This was another huge synchronicity for me, as recently I had been very called to sound healing.

The sound vibrations we used and felt were very powerful. For one exercise, we took turns sitting in the middle of the circle to receive healing. When it was my turn, I felt and saw my inner fire dragon emerge. Fire was being breathed out and all the way up through the crown out of my head. Powerful rays like the sun were shooting out of my heart center. I saw myself flying up out of my body into the outer reaches of the Universe. I could hear the word "galactic" being spoken in my mind.

When the healing was complete, Tom described some of the same visuals and said he sensed that I was a "traveler of different worlds." How wonderful to have this validation of what I'd experienced for myself!

When Farshad's turn rolled around, the image of the TRUTH tarot card from John Holland's Psychic Tarot deck flashed in my mind's eye. I saw the man in the image morph into Farshad, looking out a window into the expanse of the Universe and just beginning to see the truth of who he really is and his role here. I could see that he too was a "Star Seed" and on a path to understanding his own spiritual heritage or lineage and unique gifts – something that would continue to be shown to him over time. I remembered the message that he would serve as a "bridge" of truth and knowledge from other realms; he needed to open up the window, just a little bit at a time, to allow more truth and clarity in.

After class, I drove back to my apartment to change into my required healing garb (white blouse and black pants) and grab a quick snack; then I headed to the Healing Temple for evening service. Tonight there was no downtime as we had a steady flow of people right up to closing time.

It was so interesting to experience each individual's unique energy and see how the healing would be tailored for their specific needs. I was even inspired to allow the projection of sounds, within my mind, to them. Earlier, even before going to class, some sounds had come forth in my meditation, which had never happened before.

At the end, Barbara, the director of the healing service and temple, complimented our group, saying we were "one hundred percent tapped into Universal Energy" and that the healing sessions she'd witnessed far surpassed other healing "classes" that had been there before, which Tom also said to us earlier that day. I loved what Barbara said next:

> ***"Spirit and this Healing Temple itself arrange and orchestrate all of this. You have all been called her for a purpose. You are all meant to be here to offer your healing services because they're so needed at this time."***

## LIGHT LANGUAGE

Interestingly, I had recently recollected two "psychic" sessions I'd had about a year before starting to formally develop my psychic skills. I was guided to try a very different approach, one I'd never heard of before, in which the "reader" would offer transmissions of light and sound through her hands. One wouldn't receive the typical messaging channeled through spoken English language, but rather through this otherworldly language, which I now know to be Light Language.

In the second reading a few months later, I had signed up for a more "typical" psychic reading, but right in the middle of the session, the reader turned to me and said, "I don't normally do this, but I'm being called to bring through some light language with you. Would you be open to this?" I was game, as I always trust what comes through is for my highest good. She proceeded to use a similar sounding "language" of sounds and hand gestures that I'd had experienced previously. When this ended, she went back into her usual voice and reading style (in plain English).

So funny that I completely forgot about these instances until now, when they came to me in this downloaded remembrance seeming to connect some dots together. I realized that this clarity was perfectly timed, so I could better understand what I am now doing for others who, like me, are awakening to their path. I also offer transmissions of energy and unlocking of codes within other people in my readings and my healing sessions, even if I'm not verbalizing the light language aloud in a way they hear it. It is transforming and awakening them in ways they themselves don't necessarily see or perhaps even understand, but rather feel.

## FATED STAR SEED MEETING

Today was a day of magical unfolding like I'd never seen before. I mean, I experience synchronicities all the time, but this one topped them all.

It all started with my morning meditation. Farshad's face flashed in my mind's eye, and I received the inspiration to "pay forward" the Star Seed book I'd been gifted in Sedona. I made note of it and continued my mediation for my own guidance and alignment of energy.

Afterward, I pulled out The Akashic Tarot deck, which was perfect since I had a mentorship session scheduled later with the deck's creator, Sharon Anne Klinger! The first card I pulled, FATED MEETING, appeared to represent the meeting of my soulmate and romantic partner soon.

Awesome! It's about time, I thought.

After completing the reading, I finished getting ready for what promised to be a busy day – the last installation of the healing mastery class followed by the kick-off that evening of the afterlife-themed weekend. Raymond Moody was going to be there, as well as other prominent speakers, including Eben Alexander and his partner, Karen Newell, who I had signed up to see.

On the drive to the Dale, I thought again of the starseed book, as if being reminded by Spirit of my assigned task. After my meeting with Sharon, I would grab a coffee at the local coffeeshop, Sacred Grounds, and then check the stores on campus to see if they carried the book, though I knew the likelihood was slim considering that this book was no longer in print and could only be found used, if you were lucky. Still I decided to put out a request to the Universe and trust that all would work out the way it was meant to.

"I think the book from Sedona was meant to stay with me," I told Spirit, "so if you want me to give Farshad a copy please help me easily find it at one of the stores today. Otherwise, I'll hand over my copy, but only as the last option."

Sometimes I surprised even myself with the way I always negotiated with Spirit!

After parting ways with Sharon, I headed straight to Sacred Grounds, to find one of my sitters from last night's healing working there!

I asked how she was feeling. I also shared what I'd felt on my end – that the energy was being focused, bringing her a sense of comfort, ease, and relaxation so she could release any tension or stress she was carrying. She validated my impression, adding that when she left she was very relaxed and had a really sound night's sleep.

Then, as I waited for my order, Eben Alexander and Karen Newell walked up right behind me! They didn't stay long – after perusing the menu the decided they preferred to eat something more substantial – but it still felt like another Spirit-led "chance" encounter.

Next, I had a run-in with another woman who had come to me for healing last night. During our session, I had seen different areas of concern fill with white light and had felt/seen Archangel Michael there to assist with the healing.

"You were at my back the entire time, but I still felt the energy go exactly where it was needed," she said, adding, "You'd better continue this work because it's fucking amazing!" What a fantastic compliment, not for my ego but as confirmation that I was on the right track in pursuing this work

– and that I was receiving and transmitting healing energy as a clear channel in a way that was also clearly felt.

I grabbed my coffee and found a nice table in the corner to jot down notes on the advice Sharon had provided during my mentoring session. As I waited for my computer to boot up, I sipped my coffee and looked over at a bookshelf next to me. Wouldn't it be funny, I thought, if the starseed book was here?

I looked at a shelf above and then shifted my eyes down to the line of books right next to me and – you guessed it – there was the book!

My jaw dropped and I busted out laughing as I pulled it off the shelf (not before taking a snapshot as proof). I mean, this is not your typical you-can-find-it-at-any-bookstore kind of book. They didn't even have Ken Carey's *first more popular* starseed book. Man, Spirit was on fire today! I couldn't wait to talk to Farshad now!

I was guided to take a moment to close my eyes, tap in, and open the book to a page that would have an important message for us both. I did exactly that, and when I opened the book and read the words on the page, I was absolutely blown away. The page I had opened to gave me a direct personal response to the question I'd been contemplating for the past couple of days.

I'd been wondering about the correlation between the places I'd lived – and specifically why two of the three – the Panama Canal Zone and West Berlin – technically no longer existed. Also, I'd always been curious about the significance of two divided cities and countries that were such huge parts of my life: East/West Berlin and North/South Korea. My dad had been stationed in West Berlin, where we lived for four years, leaving only one month before the Wall came down! I remembered being in a sea of people at the Brandenburg Gate to witness President Reagan's speech – arguably his most famous – when he said, *"Mr. Gorbachev, tear down this wall!"*

In this section of the book I was guided to, Carey writes about "The Winds of Change," and specifically references the reunification of Berlin in the '80s and how this came about as a part of a wave of new consciousness and raising of awareness across the globe. I was being shown part of my purpose and pre-birth plan to be part of the wave or winds of change. I plopped myself back into my chair to let it sink in.

And now, for the grand finale of my amazing morning of synchronicities …

Not five minutes later, I glanced up, still in awe and contemplating what I'd just read and experienced, and guess who I saw standing right outside the window straight ahead of me. Farshad! He had just strolled up and stopped right by the window as he chatted with some people outside. I mean, he was literally framed, right there, directly in front of me. It could not have been more perfectly orchestrated and divinely timed. Okay, time for the official mic drop! I felt like giving Spirit a standing ovation.

After savoring this for a moment, I casually walked over to the door, greeted Farshad, and told him that when he had a minute I had an important message for him … from Spirit! He was intrigued, to say the least, and I didn't have to wait long. We found a private spot outside so I could share the unfoldment of the morning and to go over the message that had come through for him. His reply: he had hoped he'd see me here. Somehow, he *knew* that he was supposed to meet me here. By this point, I was practically floating in all the magic happening around me!

**MY STARSEED TRANSMISSION:**

***You don't need to open the door all at once;***
***It's a multistep process.***
***It starts with the initial awakening, followed by a little spark***
***of understanding, opening your eyes to the fact that***
***there's more than what you ever thought.***
***Then, you become curious and this is your momentum***

*that will lead you to the next thing and then the next inspiration or breadcrumb and so on.*

*It's all divinely orchestrated for you so that you can receive what you need at just the right timing. For example, you may read/hear/see something at one point in your life, but only so much can be absorbed or understood at that particular time. But it plants the seed. Then, when the timing is ripe, this will all click and you'll remember WITH understanding.*

*However, you CAN invite in more... if you are ready for more and want this, you can set your intention and purposely ask for us to connect with you and give you what you're ready for at that time.*

*The door/window has already been opened. And now, you can enjoy the wonder of the unfoldment. There is so much more for you to learn and see. Continue to follow your inner guidance. It will lead you to the next step. There is no such thing as coincidence.*

## LAST DAY

What an amazing week I'd had. I did not want it to end. For our last healing session, we split into groups of threes. I had just been made aware that this Healing Temple was considered an energy vortex, with its most powerful spot in the back, exactly where my group was stationed! The energy was intensified in these healings. It was so intimate and beautiful.

One of my partners was inspired to use some healing tones for our sitter, which I could feel vibrating and pulsing through me. Other groups began piping in with their harmonizing tones and within minutes it sounded like we had a whole choir of angels singing through us and around us.

When the healing was complete, my sitter shared that at one point she had looked up at me and saw an angel standing right behind me, channeling healing light through me.

Tom, our wonderful mentor, became emotional as he closed out the class. This group, he said, was the most special, sincere, open-hearted group of individuals he had ever had the honor of teaching. He was also very complimentary about the level of healing work and connection we were able to bring forward across this week. We were all emotional, brimming with love and appreciation for having been drawn here together for this sacred work. I could not have asked for a more magical, truly profound way to end the week and this part of my journey.

Looking back, I can see how all the ebbs and flows carried me through the struggles, the uncertainty, and the doubts. I can see how it was all, not just necessary, but a blessing, teaching me to celebrate the milestones, no matter how big or small, and finally reach new heights in my soul's evolution. At the same time, I knew there was so much more to come, and I looked forward to discovering what the Universe had in store for me - one step at a time.

## HIGHER HEART ACTIVATION

# DROPPING SHIELDS.
# DIVINE LOVE.
# YOUR HEART IS HEALED.

***"Through this Stargate of the heart, we have the potential to connect with Divine love, the love that exists in all things, and experience the heaven within.***

***The more you express the love you are,***
***the more it is reflected back to you.***
***Love is your truth."***

~ Gateway of Light Activation Oracle Deck by Kyle Gray

# EPILOGUE

For a while I didn't know how or when to end this story. Maybe, I thought, it would be with my return to the starting point (now the penultimate chapter), but then I realized that this was just an in-between time, a liminal space before I headed out again. I knew I'd continue keeping a journal for myself, but I couldn't keep adding to what was already more than seventeen hundred pages – my God, that would be one fucking long book! The next step was to edit it down to a manageable size, which is what you have in your hands today.

It was later, when I returned to Mount Shasta, that I received guidance to include the section on Lilydale – that was my real "coming home," as far as my soul's purpose.

Mount Shasta had been coming up intermittently for two weeks and I knew I needed to go back there. It was a safe space for me to work on the edits without distractions. In fact, this entire journey was largely meant to insulate me from outside influences that may take me off path or prevent me from moving forward.

I needed to be in places where I could allow my creativity to flow and to fully and deeply tap into the guidance from Spirit and to feel safe/secure in expressing and sharing who I really am in every possible way, without any censorship or reservation.

Coming back into the energy of Mount Shasta, the root chakra of the world, would ground me, give me a sense of security and stability, and inspire my creative writing/editing process. I also knew there were more magical meetings and synchronicities in store for me there. It certainly didn't disappoint. Not only did I complete this book, I was led to a non-stop array of amazing people, readings, healings, spirit communications, and blessings.

As I talked about in earlier chapters, my spirit team often communicates with me through electronics in order to get my undivided attention and give me direct, tangible messages... and that's exactly what happened during the editing process, when this manuscript was still very much in marinating mode. I just knew there was still some important message I wanted to add as the final ingredient, but wasn't sure what. That's when I noticed that some of the files on the desktop of my computer had been mysteriously and spontaneously moved – and their names completely changed!

As I reviewed these Spirit-inspired changes, I had a knowing that within these titles were hidden messages that I still needed to convey to connect the dots of my journey and tie everything together. They were as follows:

1: My file containing the outline for my online course on "Learning the Language of Your Soul and Unlocking the Code to your Intuitive Guidance System" had been changed to the much simpler:

**EARTH ENERGY**

The clear message here was that another key to opening up your intuitive guidance can be sourced from establishing your connection to Mother Earth energy, which is exactly what I had done while traveling to various power spots across the U.S. The vortex energy way stations my intuition led me to served as gateways that rerouted me from the winding country back roads onto a Universal highway system, so to speak, which would help to expedite, amplify, and broaden the bandwidth of my connection.

While visiting these different areas along ley lines can heighten your intuition, you don't have to go there, or anywhere, to connect. Whether you are at a vortex area in Sedona or in a busy city, the access or gateway lies within YOU, within your heart. YOU ARE THE PORTAL to connect to your higher self, your spirit family, and the Universal consciousness! However, wherever you are, finding a way to be outside on the land and in nature, building a relationship with Earth energy, will support your awakening and expansion.

2: The file previously titled "SPIRIT FILES," which housed all my audios for meditations and other recordings used in my very disciplined daily spiritual practice, had been changed to:

**PLAY, FUN!**

This rather amusing message here let me know that rather than making everything feel like work all the time, I needed to have more fun and play in my life! Allow more ease and flow and make the journey enjoyable.

Now, that doesn't completely let us off the hook with the "D" word. Some discipline is certainly needed whenever you want to learn or become more adept at something. Practice and repetition will hone your skills so that eventually, rather than feeling like you have to analyze and remember each step, it'll begin to feel more natural, and automatic. It becomes a new way of being. It's just a matter of finding balance in everything.

Remember, the point of sharing the story of my spiritual journey does not mean you have to take the same extremes I did. I am not advocating for you to now end your relationships, give away all your belongings, quit your job, live only in vortex areas, and get up at five every morning for meditation. This is simply what MY soul called ME to do at that time in my life, on my own unique soul path, which – as my guides keep telling me, is more "Galactic" in nature. YOU must tap in and find what YOUR soul is calling you toward.

Sometimes the hardest step in the process can be to just LET GO and have joy and fun along the way. Is every moment of your life going to be blissful? No, but you don't have to let the moments where you're feeling contrasting emotions (let's not even call them negative) take you down. They are meant to guide you, not hinder you. So let them flow so as not to block them; then you'll find yourself shifting into a state of allowing and realignment with your true happiness.

3: Finally, the file "StarSeed Health" had been changed to the lengthy and very specific message, as follows:

***Similar to the idea that our body is not an obstruction, but a key/gateway to connection with Source, the same is true of feeling into and experiencing emotions; they are not a hindrance nor are they to be repressed/suppressed, but are meant to be appreciated and experienced…***

**ALLOW THESE TO FLOW.**

You may recall how in the first chapter of this book, I had angrily asked my guides, "Why does it have to be so hard?" The answer? It doesn't! We make it hard because it's simply a pattern that we've become accustomed to, but now we have the opportunity to clear, release, and alchemize those old patterns and beliefs once and for all.

Often, we feel angst, confusion, or depression because we are being governed by the rules of our rational mind and logic. When we cut off the channel between our mind and our heart, we also separate ourselves from who we really are, why we came here, and from the flow of guidance and connection. And as we begin to get the channels flowing again, there may be some stops and starts at first. It may feel like a sacrifice.

There is much power in our emotions once we learn how to manage and correctly interpret them. They ARE our guidance system and offer us key information on which direction to take on our path.

We have to ***learn to discern and to start asking the right questions***. We must shift from methodically overanalyzing everything to experiencing life from a feeling standpoint. When you find yourself questioning something and getting stuck on the mental wheels of your mind, try shifting your energy down out of your head and into your heart. Then, rather than asking what the most logical thing to do is, ask yourself, ***"How does it feel and what is this emotion revealing to me now?"*** This will begin to bring you the clarity you actually seek that your mind alone cannot provide.

Some other questions I often pose to myself include:

- ~ *How can I see this through a different lens?*
- ~ *What are some other creative possibilities and potentials to consider?*
- ~ *Does this feel in alignment with my soul?*

And as best-selling author, spiritual life coach and quantum optimist, Cynthia Sue Larson would remind us to ask as we begin to shift our perspective and open our hearts to new possibilities:

***"How good can it get?"***

Then rather than forcing an immediate solution or clear answer, let the questions flow out to the Universe and expect to be shown evidence of movement in the perfect divine timing. You can't just read a manual or book to understand how your emotional guidance system works. It takes actually experiencing things and the feelings that go along with them.

It's not about choosing mind over emotion, or the other way around. The KEY to opening the door to your creative power and intuition is bridging the two together, creating a channel between your mind and your heart and bringing consciousness into the equation.

I understand what it's like to feel overwhelmed and even trapped by your emotions and therefore wanting to block them as much as possible. Experiences in my youth had pulled me down into such dark depths of despair, and as a result I'd lived much of my life in my head. My emotions were like the proverbial can of worms, and I kept a tight lid on it for fear of falling back down that dark well I had barely escaped before. What I finally realized was that by blocking myself off from experiencing my "negative" emotions, I was simultaneously blocking myself off from feeling happiness.

As challenging as it can be to LET GO and ALLOW the feelings that come up along the path, it's necessary. We have to release, surrender, and let go to allow the channel of healing energy, guidance, love, and connection to flow through us and to us.

***Your joy and your capacity to love is your greatest superhuman power here and your heart is the gateway. Open the gate and allow yourself in!***

Spirit didn't stop with the electronic confirmations. At the exact moment I was writing this epilogue with the downloaded message to ***KEEP THE FAUCET OF OUR EMOTIONS RUNNING***, the water in my rental literally shut off! I turned the sink handle to the on position so I would know as soon as it came back on. Thankfully, only minutes later it was flowing at full blast.

I knew from past experience that I had to let the water run and flush itself for a few minutes to clear any contaminants or harmful buildup that often comes when it's been sitting stagnant in the pipes. As I observed this whole process unfolding, I knew in an instant that this synchronicity was all orchestrated by Spirit as a perfect real-life and real-time analogy to illustrate the point they wanted me to convey. My team knows how much I like to have crystal-clear messaging and tangible evidence to solidify and confirm the guidance I'm receiving... and they never disappoint!

This manifestation was a direct reflection of what I had experienced on my journey with all the emotional baggage that had blocked my pipes and needed to be flushed from my system. I had to go through some spiritual healing and detox in order to clear my pathways so I could accurately use and interpret my emotional guidance system the way it was designed to work. Furthermore, stuff comes up when we're undergoing the spiritual awakening and ascension process.

The more I let go and allowed the flow to carry any mental, physical, and emotional debris to the surface, the more I allowed my spiritual guidance and confidence to grow... and the easier and more enjoyable the path became.

Well, the very same messages that came through to help me along my journey are now meant for you. If you've shut off the faucet in your own life, it's time to turn it back on and then, as my guides have repeatedly told me:

***KEEP THE FAUCET RUNNING!***

As if the sequence of earlier messages and synchronicities wasn't already clear enough, I pulled two oracle cards and received the following affirmations.

The first card (which had actually shown up two days in a row) was **"FLOW,"** from John Holland's *The Psychic Tarot for the Heart* deck. In fact its card number ten in this deck not only aligned with the ending of this book, but the end of a cycle. Endings always lead to new beginnings!

The second card – *Higher Heart Activation* from Kyle Gray's *Gateway of Light Activation Oracle* deck – perfectly aligned with the message of creating a bridge between your mind and heart.

***"Through this Stargate of the heart, we have the potential to connect with Divine love, the love that exists in all things, and experience the heaven within...***
***The more you express the love you are,***
***the more it is reflected back to you.***
***Love is your truth."***

I'm usually a super private person, but I will always share openly and honestly when I feel there is some value and purpose to it. From Day 1 of this journey, my spirit team urged me to document my experiences, and I did so as if no one would ever read it. Honestly, I didn't see how I could possibly share such intimate raw details with the world.

Slowly, I was given more and more courage, and the softening of my resistance, to open up and allow my true self, with all the imperfections and crazy, unbelievable parts of my life, to be revealed. I know there are so many others going through a similar experience and are looking for guidance, feeling stuck, and trying to find their true path in life. It is my hope that the story of my unique path will inspire you to be, embody, and fully embrace your unique self without apologies.

**BRIDGE OF THE WORLD AND THE HEART OF THE UNIVERSE**

Just when I thought it was time to close this book, there was one more perfectly timed nugget of guidance that was dropped into my awareness. I had long been aware of, and fascinated by, the correlation between my life and divided countries – Panama, Germany, and Korea. While in Lilydale for my Fated Meetings, I was lined up with a second copy of the hard-to-get-your-hands-on Starseeds book and guided to the exact page and chapter on "Winds of Change," which talks about the reunification of Berlin. This shed light on why I had been strategically positioned, not only to witness this event, but add my own energetic influence and ingredient to the melting pot towards a more positive outcome.

Well, as one final synchronicity for this book which I get a very strong feeling will connect the dots to the next chapter of my ongoing spiritual journey, as I've never stopped traveling, searching, and exploring and receiving more channeled information and guidance in a clearer and clearer way, I experienced the following.

Later along my journey, I had landed in Minneapolis, where I was staying while finishing up the final edits. It was then that I had an in-person reading with Michael, the amazing psychic who had given me such incredible guidance at the beginning of my travels. Now, Michael passed on the critical message from my Spirit Guides that there was still something else I was supposed to integrate into the book. I was to ***open the channel of my heart*** while teaching and encouraging my readers to tap into the flow of their own emotions and intuition. I had the feeling for a long time that there was still some missing component that needed to be added, but even as he passed on this message I wondered exactly how I was supposed to do that! I thought back to the many vulnerable and emotionally heart-wrenching moments that were already sprinkled throughout the entire story and I wondered what more Spirit wanted me to convey or allow.

The very next day, I experienced a series of synchronicities, as well as the downloaded messages I mentioned earlier in this epilogue. Thanks, Spirit! I thought as I sent the revisions to my publishing team.

Apparently, there was still something more to uncover....

The following morning, I woke to the recollection of a profound dream message.

## Dream Tarot

I'm shown a card with a moving image in which I'm walking alone at night at the top of a hill. It appears to be decorated for a party as there are hanging lights and colorful heart shaped streamers of purples, reds, and pinks. It looks beautiful, but I feel sad because I feel alone here without a romantic partner to share this experience with. The streamers are waving in the wind like colorful Tibetan prayer flags and take on the appearance of a web or larger fabric of sorts.

Then, while still in my dream state and observing this imagery, an inner voice clearly shared the meaning as follows:

***The love you seek outside of yourselves is too expansive to solely fit in such a small box as in one individual or one romantic partner. It is so much greater.***

***It is embedded all around you in the fabric of all creation. Your DNA and all the cells of your body vibrate with the frequency of pure love.***

***Go within. Connect to the gateway of your heart and you will connect to the true Source of the greater love you seek.***

***CONNECT TO THE HEART OF THE UNIVERSE***

Upon waking with this powerful dream message still ringing through me, I was taken back to my earliest childhood memories in which I had essentially allowed myself to be reprogrammed to the frequency of disconnection, abandonment, unworthiness, and fear. AND SO, the more I believed this, the more it was clearly reflected back to me in every kind of relationship. I was also reminded of this documented soul journey, now a few years past, in which I'd often focused my desire on a romantic partner. And though it wasn't unreasonable, it was very limiting in that the force that was ultimately driving my desire was the search for a Divine and Universal connection.

Then, after allowing this wisdom to fully sink in and completing my meditation, per my usual ritual, I sat up in bed, put in my earbuds, and opened my phone's Google app to pull up an inspirational video to listen to while making coffee. As I pulled up the internet search engine, the usual suggested news headliners were lined up on the page below. I usually don't give them a second look, but on this day, the first headline caught my eye with the title:

**"The Heart of the Universe"**

My eyes widened at the exact wording from my dream message as well as the "heart" theme, which had been my spirit team's urging as a critical message for both me and for the closing of this book. However, as quickly as the article appeared on the suggested Google links, it disappeared, and all new links and titles took its place! Quickly, I scrambled to type in the exact title in the search engine in hopes that I could find the very same news article. What pulled up were links to Marvel comics that included those keywords – not at all what I was searching for. I removed the word marvel, which had been added without my approval, but still no luck. Even as I made this last-ditch effort I wondered why I felt so compelled to lay eyes on this particular article. Well, there was only one way to find out.

I added the word "news" to the search engine, since the link that magically flashed before me appeared to be a news article. When I saw the first option that appeared on my screen, my jaw dropped. The article was titled **"The Heart of the Universe: How the Panama Canal Changed the World."** [2*]

My heart skipped a beat as I learned that the slogan "The Land Divided, The World United" once appeared on the seal of the waterway. Also, the Panama Canal had served as "a national symbol with international reach

2* Korn, Jennifer. CNN (January 19, 2025). "The Heart of the Universe: How the Panama Canal Changed the World."

as symbolized in the country's coat of arms which says: *pro mundi beneficio* — "for the benefit of the world."

In an Akashic reading I'd gifted myself only a couple of years earlier, I had asked the same question about the significance of the Panama Canal in my soul's plan. Just as I had left Berlin, Germany only a month before their reunification, draft agreements were already in process when I was born there. President Jimmy Carter began negotiating the return of control of the canal to Panama one year later. I often wondered about the timing with which I lived in these key places at pivotal times in history. During my reading, it was shared that I was specifically placed in this area to offer a sort of balancing energy for this fragile vortex area. When searching for more information on my own, however, none was to be found. I had always been drawn to the history of my birthplace and felt that the story here was not yet finished. That something full circle would be coming about. Same goes for Korea, which is obviously still divided.

My guides wanted to be sure that THIS specific connection was delivered to me just in the nick of time as it was chock full of meaning and magnitude that has yet to be played out and revealed to us all. But I can't think of a better analogy to their previously repeated messages on exactly what each of us can do, both individually and collectively, as we ride the waves and learn to navigate the winds of change.

The Panama Canal, which has been affected by severe drought, is such a perfect reflection for the state of the world right now where collectively the channel to our heart chakra is desperately begging for our attention to turn the faucet back on and get the water flowing again. No system is isolated...each impacts the other...they are all connected and have global implications. Blockage issues with one water source will lead to issues with other major waterways, and so forth. It reminds me of how in college, while on assignment for a semester in the Southwest, I studied riparian areas (i.e., areas of land that border bodies of water, such as rivers, streams, lakes, and ponds – waterways!) – and how just one seemingly insignificant negative impact in these delicate ecosystems can have rippling ramifications downstream.

Now, as I contemplated the significance of this time in history, I wondered whether in my lifetime I will have the opportunity to witness the manifestation resulting from these powerful winds of change where a land once divided can become a "World United." A time in which humanity will gain a better understanding of who we are, why we're here, and shed light on our place in the Universe to include more conscious connection with worlds beyond this physical realm.

All I know is, I am eager and excited to see what unfolds! We're all in this together and apparently, it can't be reiterated or emphasized enough:

***THE KEY IS TO OPEN THE CHANNEL OF YOUR HEART***

Ultimately, the takeaway is that our soul journey never ends – even after our spirit leaves the physical body. We just continue onto another adventure, tapping into our inner compass to lead the way, rather than giving our power and freedom away to others around us.

As it turns out, the "FATED MEETING" I had was not just with Farshad, but Tom, our entire healing group, Michael, and everyone I was divinely guided to along my journey, including my amazing publishing team: Shanda, owner of Transcendent Publishing, and my fantastic editor, Dana, who just so happens to also be a psychic medium and offers intuitive messages and communication from loved ones! Of course, the most important fated meeting of all was with my Higher Self. And since that time the journey has been a non-stop unfolding of new places, adventures, relationships, spirit communications, insights, and "close encounters," which I look forward to sharing soon.

Spiritual awakening is the process of waking up from the illusion of the "reality" we see around us and past any limitations, self-imposed or otherwise. It is opening yourself to new possibilities for your life, discovering your purpose, and tapping into your creative power and potential, which is infinite.

Intuitive/psychic, mediumistic, and healing gifts are not reserved for a small "chosen" few. They are innate to every single human. However, it is up to YOU to open these gifts that have been bestowed upon you and to do the spiritual work to exercise and apply them. Make no mistake, spiritual development is not the easiest path, but it is the most rewarding one. And, like the butterfly effect, everything you do to open yourself up to your soul's purpose has a positive impact on everyone and everything around you. We are all part of this Universal web that we are simultaneously creating and weaving together.

When you feel dissatisfaction or a longing for something different in your life, that is the soul spark within you urging you to wake up and move in a new direction, whatever that looks like for you. Your soul is calling you... are you ready to listen?

***You are so much more powerful than you know.  
This is the time to awaken to the remembrance of  
who you really are and  
tap into your own power and potential.***

Of this you can be sure: once you decide to step onto this path, magic will unfold for you in so many unexpected ways beyond your wildest imagination. I hope to see you along the way. I get the sense that my story, my journey, has just begun!

## FOLLOW YOUR INTUITION… IT WILL GUIDE YOU, ALWAYS.

*The road is long and may be dark and rocky at times,*
*but you will always be guided and you're never alone.*
*You have a whole team ready to help you…*
*all you have to do is ask.*

*MAY YOU TRUST IN YOURSELF,*
*MOVE PAST YOUR FEARS,*
*HAVE THE COURAGE*

*TO STEP OUT ONTO YOUR OWN SOUL'S JOURNEY*
*AND TO FULFILL YOUR OWN SOUL'S PURPOSE.*

*In the end,*
*All roads lead within*
*To face your innermost thoughts and feelings*
*Towards healing and expansion*
*On my way to becoming*
*Who you really are*
*Who you've really always been.*

*On the other side of the door*
*that you're locking out*
*is your path,*
*your purpose,*
*DIVINE help*
*and so much growth and abundance*
*JUST WAITING FOR YOU…*
*let it in*

# ABOUT THE AUTHOR

Jennifer Vroom is a Communication Expert, Intuitive, Teacher of Consciousness and Meditation, Energy Healing Channel, and Spirit Inspired Artist.

With a master's degree in Speech Language Pathology, she has over 25 years of experience teaching, speaking, and working with clients and professionals internationally in the areas of communication, meditation, and mindfulness.

It wasn't until much later in her career that she fully realized why she'd been guided to go into the field of communication. She is now able to apply her plethora of knowledge and expertise to serve as a strong bridge for telepathic spirit communication and energy work.

Jennifer empowers clients to tap into their own intuitive guidance and unique soul gifts while guiding them through their spiritual awakening and healing. Her mission is to teach, uplift and inspire others on the journey of remembering their soul's purpose and embodying their full power and potential.

You can find out more about her current offerings and connect with her by visiting:

www.jennifervroom.com

www.ingramcontent.com/pod-product-compliance
Lightning Source LLC
Chambersburg PA
CBHW051608120626
46551CB00014B/1720
* 9 7 9 8 9 9 2 2 2 0 7 6 6 *